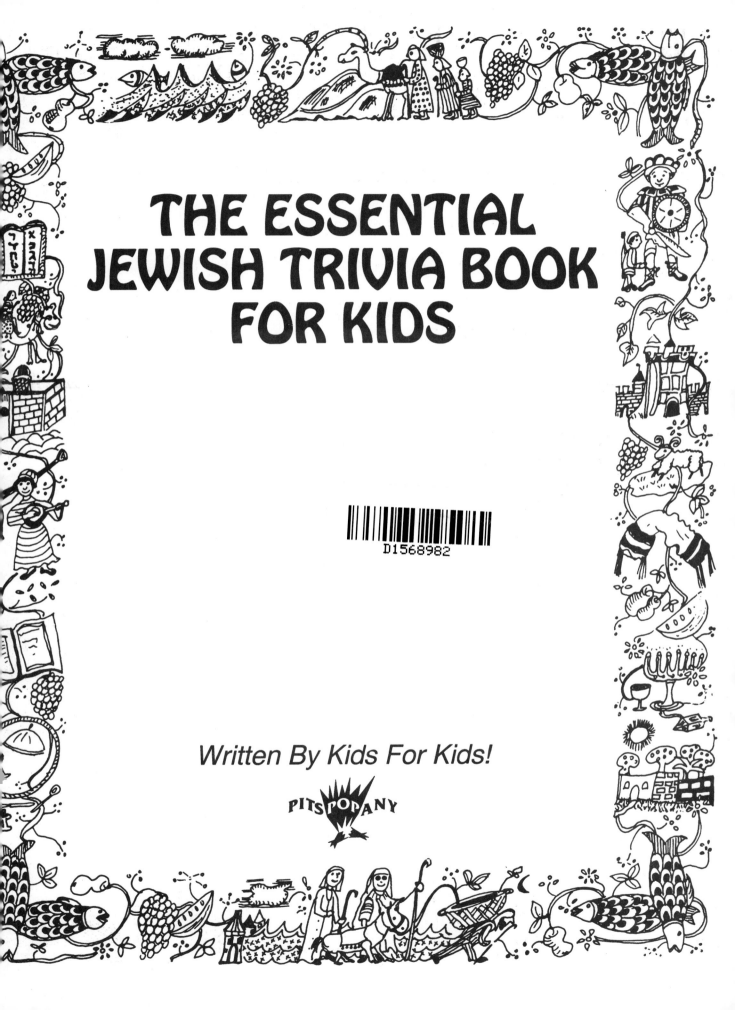

THE ESSENTIAL JEWISH TRIVIA BOOK FOR KIDS

Written By Kids For Kids!

PITSPOPANY

ISBN: 0-943706-29-7

PITSPOPANY PRESS books may be purchased for educational or
special sales by contacting:
Marketing Director, Pitspopany Press, 40 East 78th Street, New York,
New York, 10021. Fax: 212 472-6253

Printed in The United States of America

Dedicated to the beloved memory of

JOSEPH PETERSEIL
"The Candy Man"

He sweetened the lives of thousands of children in shul, who took candy from his hands and love from his heart.

His memory will endure in them and in us.

Esther Peterseil

Yaacov and Tamar Peterseil -
Tehila, Gedalia, Shlomo, Nachum, Tiferet, Temima, Yosef, Todahya, Tanya

Andrew and Dorothy Tananbaum -
Zoe, JoBeth, Tanner

Table of Contents

ESSENTIAL TRIVIA?

If you're an adult you probably smiled when you read the title of this book: **THE ESSENTIAL JEWISH TRIVIA BOOK FOR KIDS**. If you're a kid you probably didn't.

We know this is true because when we showed the cover to people almost all the adults smiled when they first saw the title. Not so the kids. So we asked ourselves, why don't kids *get* the oxymoron in the title, the obvious contradiction of the words "essential" and "trivia"?

And we came up with a theory. It's got to do with Jewish identity, or rather the lack of it. For most Jewish kids the key word in the title is "trivia" because the questions found inside this book are facts they don't know. They're trivia, in much the same way someone might say that knowing the distance from the earth to the moon is trivia. After all, unless you're a physicist or astronomer, or work for NASA, when would you ever need to use this information? Similarly, if you're not actively in touch at some level with your Jewish heritage why would these questions be anything more than "trivia"?

And that, believe it or not, is good for marketing.

Kids love to amaze their friends with esoteric knowledge, trivial facts that others don't know. That's why kids pick up this book at bookstores much more readily than their parents. They look through the book and say, "Wow! I never knew that!" And a sale is made.

But that's also the problem.

For while most parents consider a substantial number of the questions inside this book "essential" to Jewish knowledge, too many kids are so far removed from their heritage that they consider these questions trivial to their everyday lives.

So we asked *kids* to write the questions and answers in this book; kids from Jewish Day Schools, Hebrew Schools, and Yeshivot. But when we asked them for questions, we asked for essential questions about Judaism, not trivia questions. We asked them for information that they already knew. In that way we would be sure to get questions that would be interesting to other kids and not questions *we* thought would be important to know. The questions are from other kids who know something about their Judaism and want to share it.

That's what makes this book important.

THE ESSENTIAL JEWISH TRIVIA BOOK FOR KIDS helps kids understand how Jews have influenced the world. It makes learning about Judaism enjoyable and entertaining. And, far from being a book on the trivial in Judaism, it touches the very roots of the Jewish people and helps make the heritage of Judaism accessible to kids.

So, if you picked up this book and didn't smile at our title, read it through.

It's never too late to smile.

Famous Jewish Men and Women

1. Which Talmudic character slept for 70 years?

2. The Arabs trace their ancestry to which Biblical character?

3. Who was the Jewish advisor to King Ferdinand & Queen Isabella?

4. Which Jewish baseball player spoke 12 languages?

5. Which Israeli prime minister was born in Kiev, Russia?

6. Name the Jewish woman astronaut who died when the space shuttle "Challenger" exploded?

1. Honi Ha-Meaggel
2. Ishmael
3. Isaac Abarbanel
4. Morris (Moe) Berg
5. Golda Meir
6. Judith Resnick

1. Which two scientists are credited with the discovery of the Polio Vaccine?

2. Who started and coached the Harlem Globetrotters?

3. Who invented the Polaroid Land Camera?

4. Who wrote the poem engraved on the Statue of Liberty?

5. Name one Jewish baseball star who refused to play on Yom Kippur.

6. Which Russian refusenik was elected to the Israeli Knesset?

1. Dr. Jonas Salk and Dr. Albert Sabin
2. Abe Saperstein
3. Edwin Land
4. Emma Lazarus
5. Hank Greenburg or Sandy Koufax
6. Natan Sharansky

1. Which Israeli war hero was also an archaeologist?

2. Which family became famous bankers in the 19th Century?

3. Who was known as the quarterback who "never made a mistake"?

4. Who founded the Chassidic movement?

5. What well known Jewish philosopher wrote, "The Lonely Man of Faith" and "On Repentance"?

6. Who was known as the "Jewish Babe Ruth"?

1. Yigal Yadin
2. The House of Rothschild
3. Sid Luckman
4. The Ba'al Shem Tov
5. Rabbi Joseph B. Soloveitchik
6. Andy Cohen

1. Which famous 19th century Jew was commodore of the U.S. Navy?

2. Who founded the Zionist movement?

3. Which famous Jewish girl won a beauty contest and was offered half a kingdom?

4. What do Isaac Stern, Yasha Heifetz and Yitzchak Perlman have in common?

5. Which football player was known as the "Rabbi"?

6. Who was Abraham's nephew?

6. Lot
5. Randy Grossman
4. They are all great violinists
3. Esther
2. Theodor Herzl
1. Uriah P. Levy

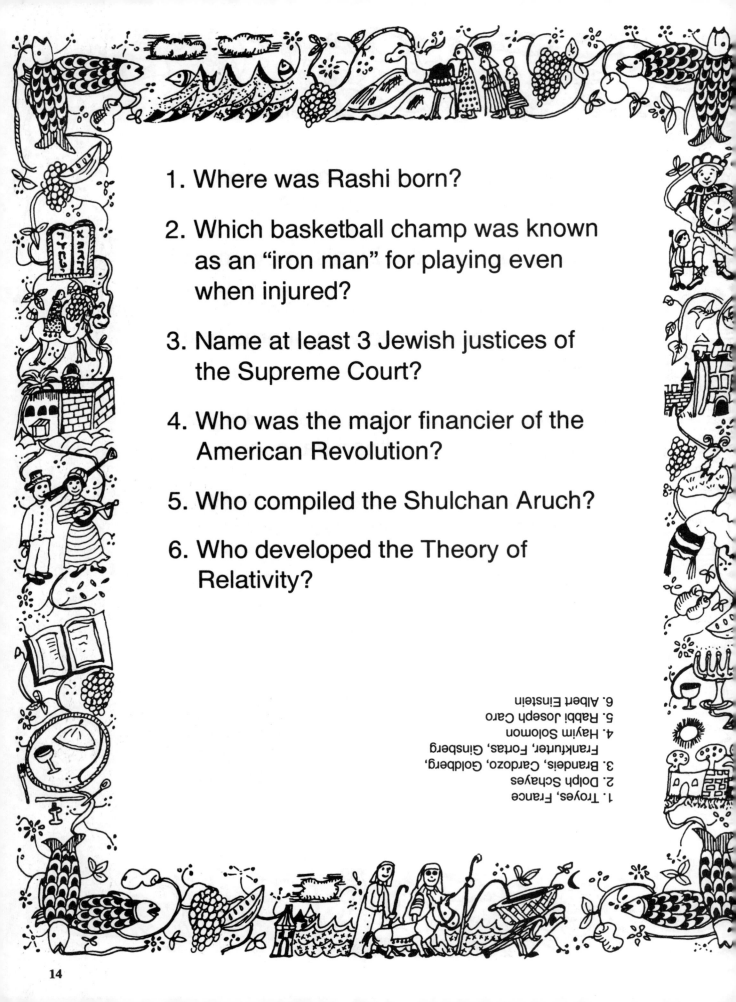

1. Where was Rashi born?

2. Which basketball champ was known as an "iron man" for playing even when injured?

3. Name at least 3 Jewish justices of the Supreme Court?

4. Who was the major financier of the American Revolution?

5. Who compiled the Shulchan Aruch?

6. Who developed the Theory of Relativity?

1. Troyes, France
2. Dolph Schayes
3. Brandeis, Cardozo, Goldberg, Frankfurter, Fortas, Ginsberg
4. Hayim Solomon
5. Rabbi Joseph Caro
6. Albert Einstein

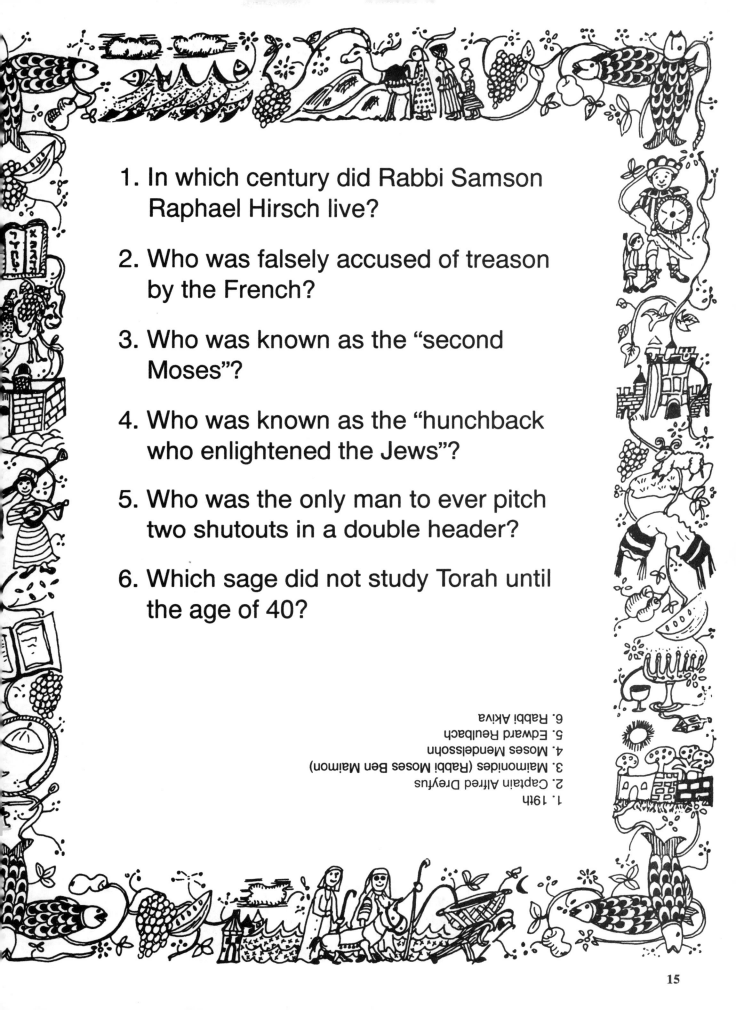

1. In which century did Rabbi Samson Raphael Hirsch live?

2. Who was falsely accused of treason by the French?

3. Who was known as the "second Moses"?

4. Who was known as the "hunchback who enlightened the Jews"?

5. Who was the only man to ever pitch two shutouts in a double header?

6. Which sage did not study Torah until the age of 40?

1. 19th
2. Captain Alfred Dreyfus
3. Maimonides (Rabbi Moses Ben Maimon)
4. Moses Mendelssohn
5. Edward Reulbach
6. Rabbi Akiva

1. Who was the second king of Israel?

2. What great Rabbi had a sandwich named after him?

3. What was the popular title of Rabbi Elijah of Vilna?

4. Name the first president of Israel?

5. How many medals did Mark Spitz win in the 1973 Olympics?

6. Which evil practice did the Chofetz Chaim preach against?

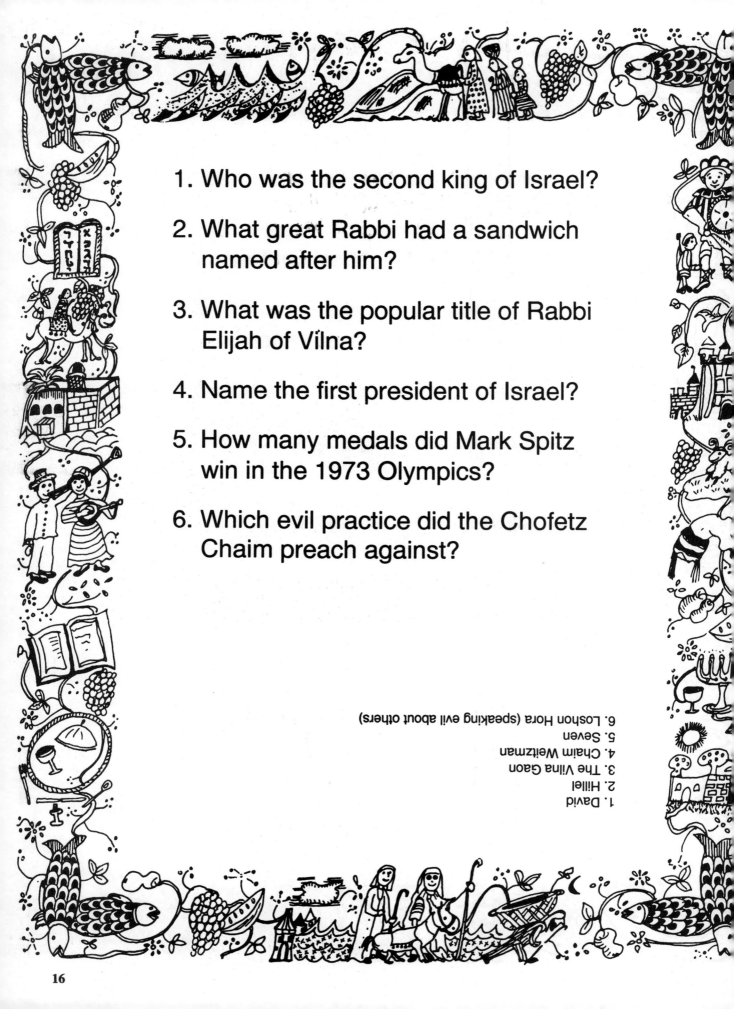

1. David
2. Hillel
3. The Vilna Gaon
4. Chaim Weitzman
5. Seven
6. Loshon Hora (speaking evil about others)

1. In the Book of Ruth, who were Naomi's daughters-in-law?

2. Which Chief Rabbi of Israel was also the Chief Rabbi of Ireland?

3. Which author of "Night" and "Dawn" also won the Nobel Peace Prize?

4. Which American Jew designed the most famous pair of jeans?

5. Which famous 19th century British Lord wore a *kipah*?

6. What controversial Jewish sports announcer was born with the name Howard Cohen?

1. Orpah, Ruth
2. Isaac Herzog
3. Elie Wiesel
4. Levi Strauss
5. Sir Moses Montefiore
6. Howard Cosell

1. Who led the last Jewish rebellion against Rome?

2. What Jew is the world's most famous mime?

3. Who was Israel's top tennis pro?

4. Who painted the 12 tribes on the stained glass windows at the Haddasah Hospital in Jerusalem?

5. Which 4 brothers made funny movies in the '30's and '40's?

6. Which famous Jewish historian wrote a history of the destruction of the Second Temple during Roman times?

1. Bar Kochba
2. Marcel Marceau
3. Amos Mansdorf
4. Marc Chagall
5. The Marx Brothers
6. Josephus

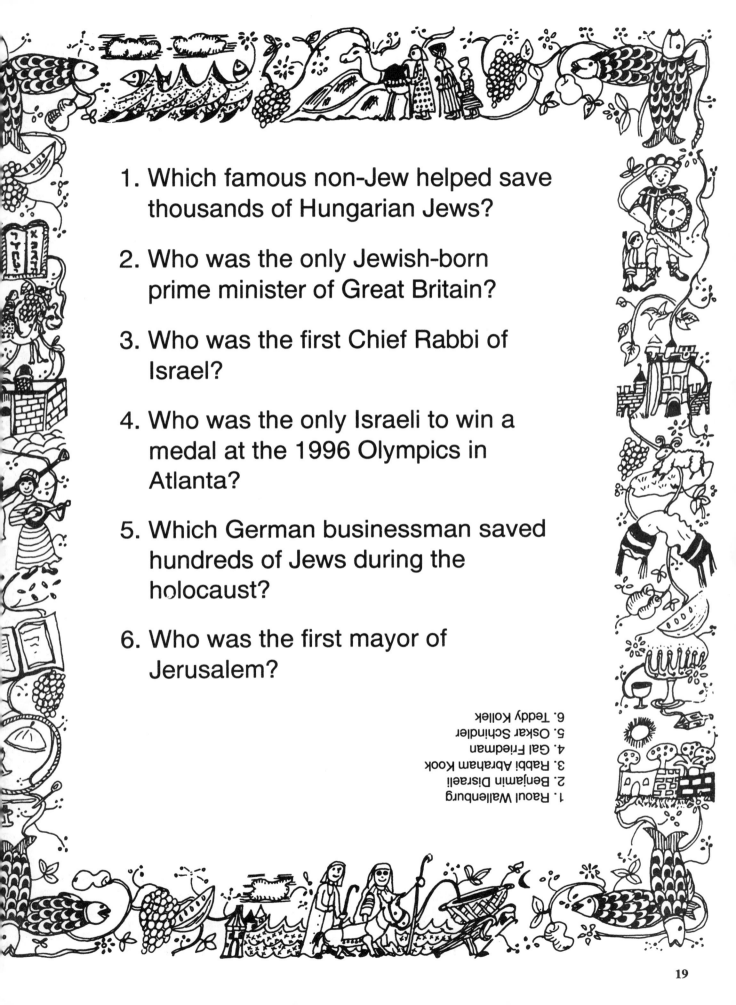

1. Which famous non-Jew helped save thousands of Hungarian Jews?

2. Who was the only Jewish-born prime minister of Great Britain?

3. Who was the first Chief Rabbi of Israel?

4. Who was the only Israeli to win a medal at the 1996 Olympics in Atlanta?

5. Which German businessman saved hundreds of Jews during the holocaust?

6. Who was the first mayor of Jerusalem?

1. Raoul Wallenburg
2. Benjamin Disraeli
3. Rabbi Abraham Kook
4. Gal Friedman
5. Oskar Schindler
6. Teddy Kollek

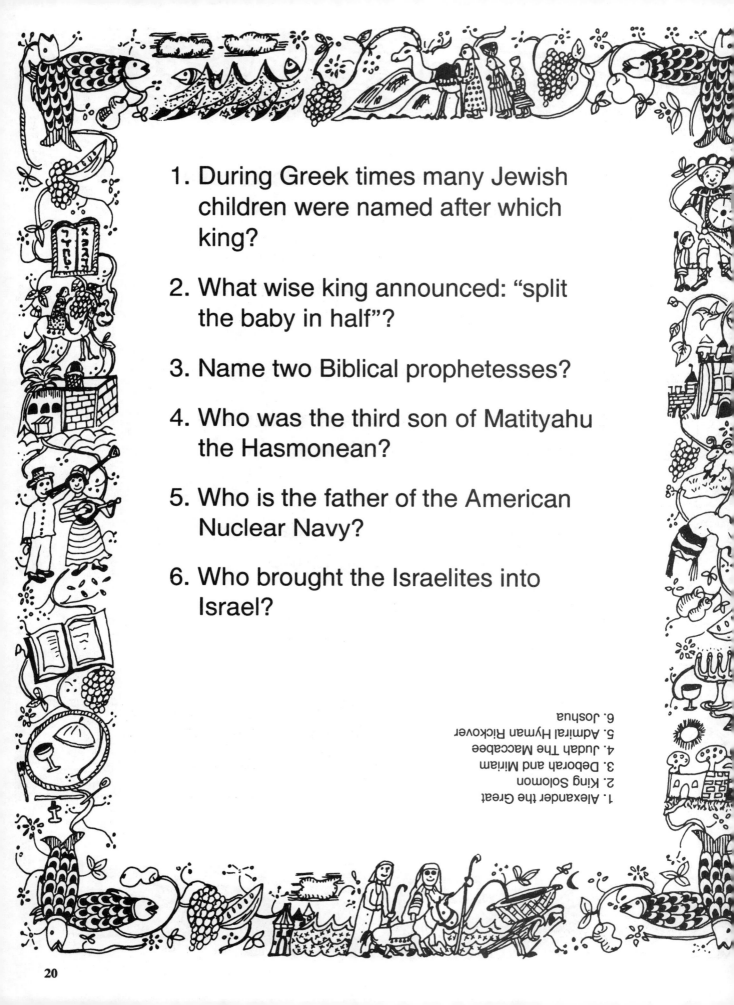

1. During Greek times many Jewish children were named after which king?

2. What wise king announced: "split the baby in half"?

3. Name two Biblical prophetesses?

4. Who was the third son of Matityahu the Hasmonean?

5. Who is the father of the American Nuclear Navy?

6. Who brought the Israelites into Israel?

1. Alexander the Great
2. King Solomon
3. Deborah and Miriam
4. Judah The Maccabee
5. Admiral Hyman Rickover
6. Joshua

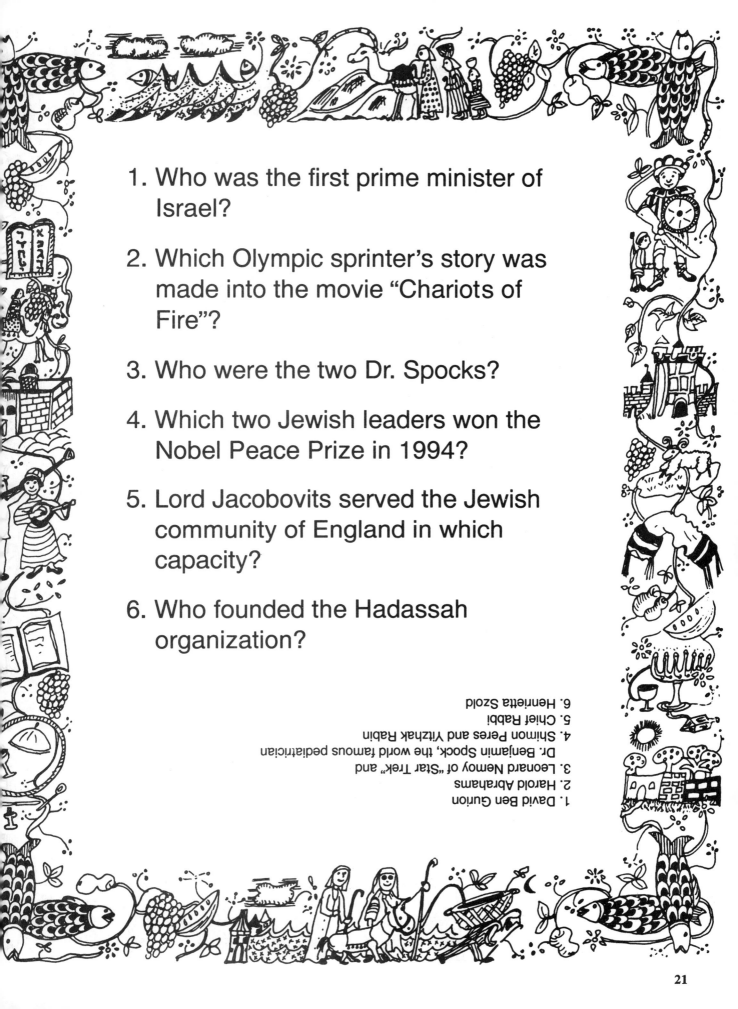

1. Who was the first prime minister of Israel?

2. Which Olympic sprinter's story was made into the movie "Chariots of Fire"?

3. Who were the two Dr. Spocks?

4. Which two Jewish leaders won the Nobel Peace Prize in 1994?

5. Lord Jacobovits served the Jewish community of England in which capacity?

6. Who founded the Hadassah organization?

1. David Ben Gurion
2. Harold Abrahams
3. Leonard Nemoy of "Star Trek" and Dr. Benjamin Spock, the world famous pediatrician
4. Shimon Peres and Yitzhak Rabin
5. Chief Rabbi
6. Henrietta Szold

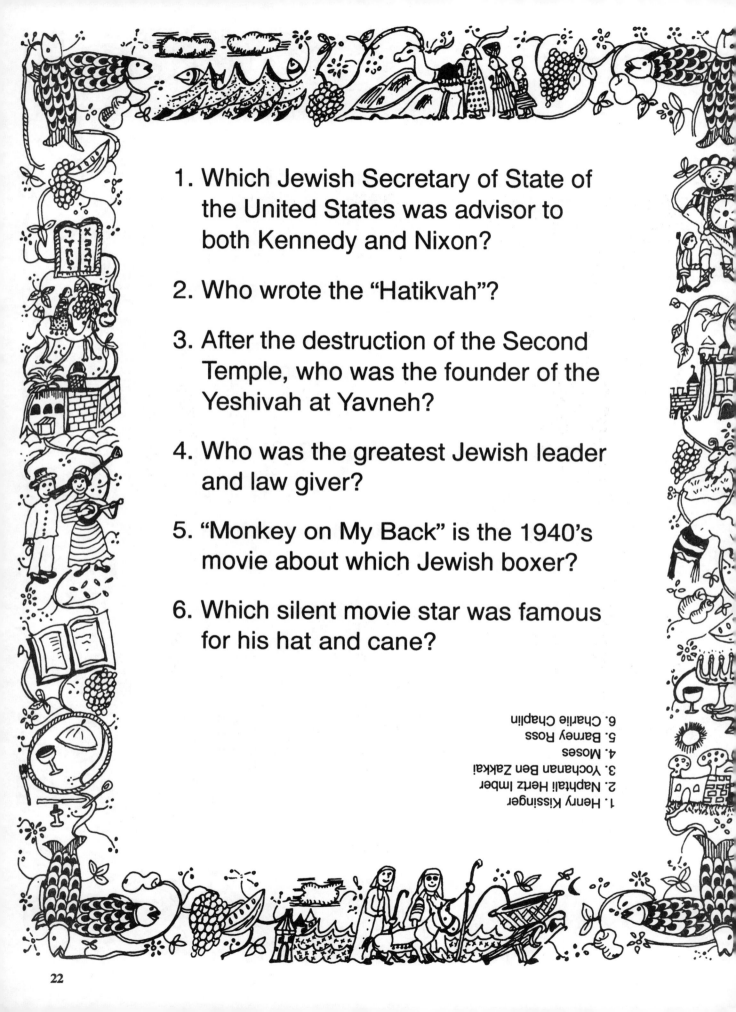

1. Which Jewish Secretary of State of the United States was advisor to both Kennedy and Nixon?

2. Who wrote the "Hatikvah"?

3. After the destruction of the Second Temple, who was the founder of the Yeshivah at Yavneh?

4. Who was the greatest Jewish leader and law giver?

5. "Monkey on My Back" is the 1940's movie about which Jewish boxer?

6. Which silent movie star was famous for his hat and cane?

1. Henry Kissinger
2. Naphtali Hertz Imber
3. Yochanan Ben Zakkai
4. Moses
5. Barney Ross
6. Charlie Chaplin

Bible

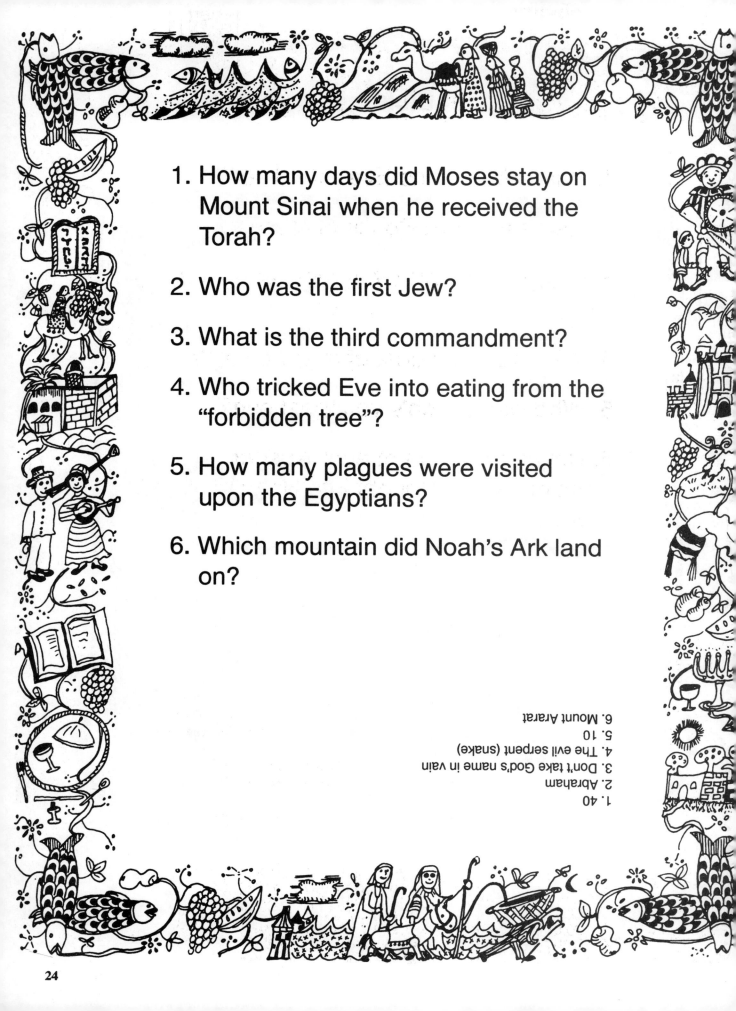

1. How many days did Moses stay on Mount Sinai when he received the Torah?

2. Who was the first Jew?

3. What is the third commandment?

4. Who tricked Eve into eating from the "forbidden tree"?

5. How many plagues were visited upon the Egyptians?

6. Which mountain did Noah's Ark land on?

1. 40
2. Abraham
3. Don't take God's name in vain
4. The evil serpent (snake)
5. 10
6. Mount Ararat

1. Name Adam and Eve's third son?

2. Name the Five Books of Moses?

3. How many days did it rain during the flood?

4. Who wore the coat of many colors?

5. Who was Jacob's youngest son?

6. How many pairs of each kosher animal were brought into Noah's Ark?

1. Seth
2. Genesis, Exodus, Leviticus, Numbers and Deuteronomy
3. 40
4. Joseph
5. Benjamin
6. 7

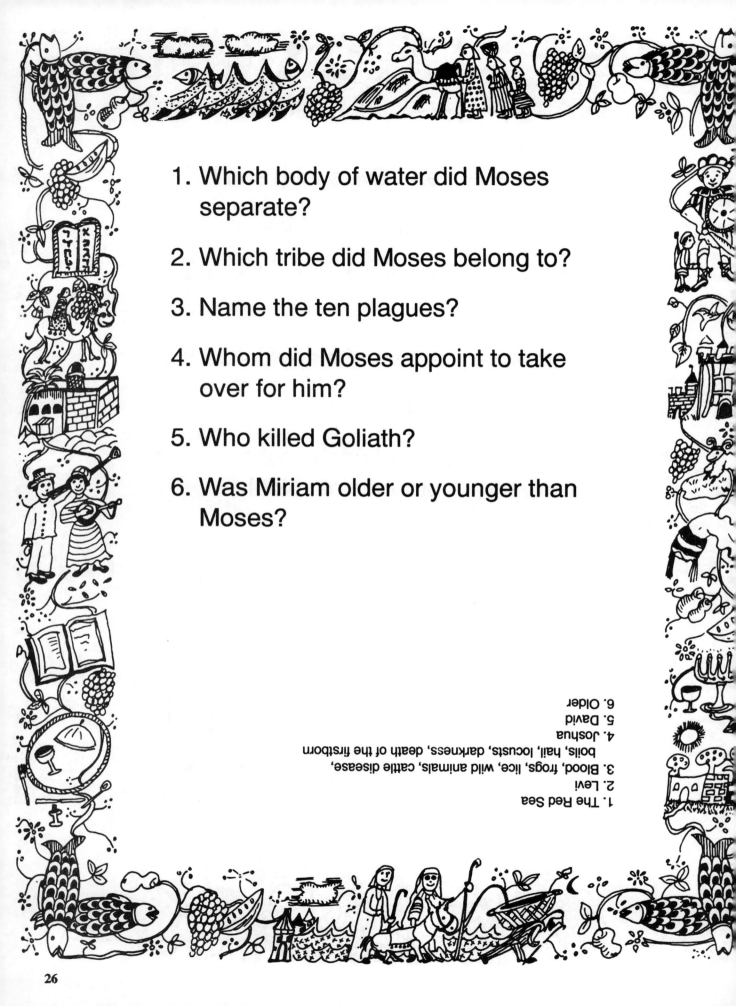

1. Which body of water did Moses separate?

2. Which tribe did Moses belong to?

3. Name the ten plagues?

4. Whom did Moses appoint to take over for him?

5. Who killed Goliath?

6. Was Miriam older or younger than Moses?

6. Older
5. David
4. Joshua
3. Blood, frogs, lice, wild animals, cattle disease, boils, hail, locusts, darkness, death of the firstborn
2. Levi
1. The Red Sea

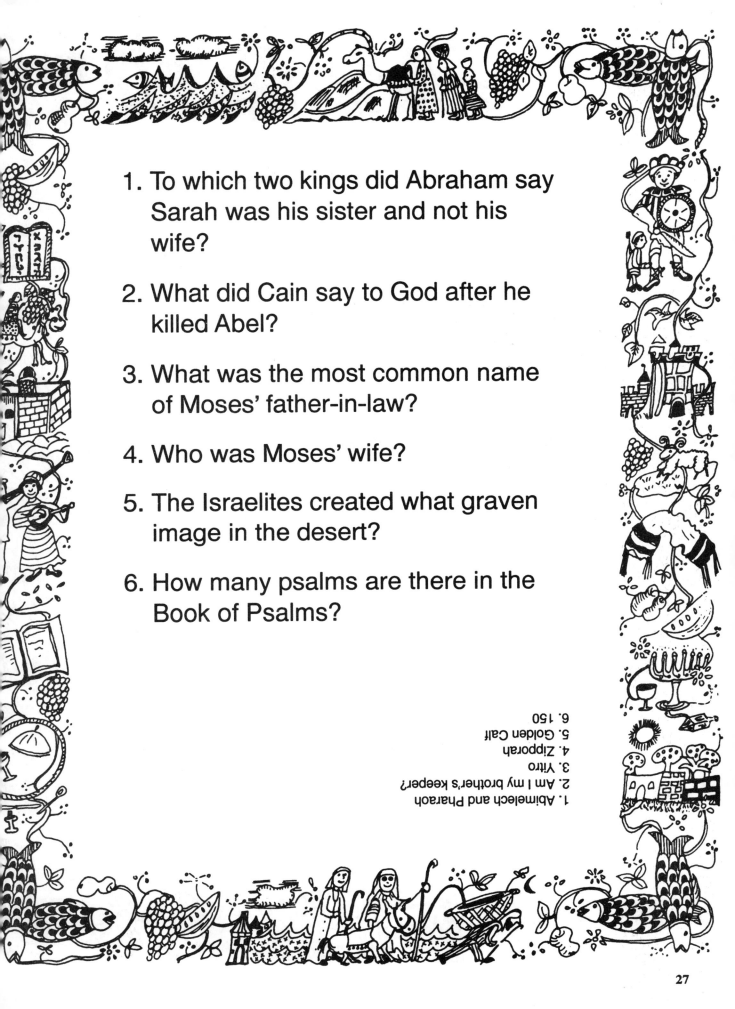

1. To which two kings did Abraham say Sarah was his sister and not his wife?

2. What did Cain say to God after he killed Abel?

3. What was the most common name of Moses' father-in-law?

4. Who was Moses' wife?

5. The Israelites created what graven image in the desert?

6. How many psalms are there in the Book of Psalms?

1. Abimelech and Pharaoh
2. Am I my brother's keeper?
3. Yitro
4. Zipporah
5. Golden Calf
6. 150

1. How many spies did Moses send into Canaan?

2. Who was Joshua's father?

3. What were the names of Isaac's two sons?

4. Who was Ishmael's mother?

5. Which two matriarchs had the same father and same husband?

6. By what title were many of the kings of Egypt known?

6. Pharaoh
5. Rachel and Leah
4. Hagar
3. Jacob and Esav
2. Nun
1. 12

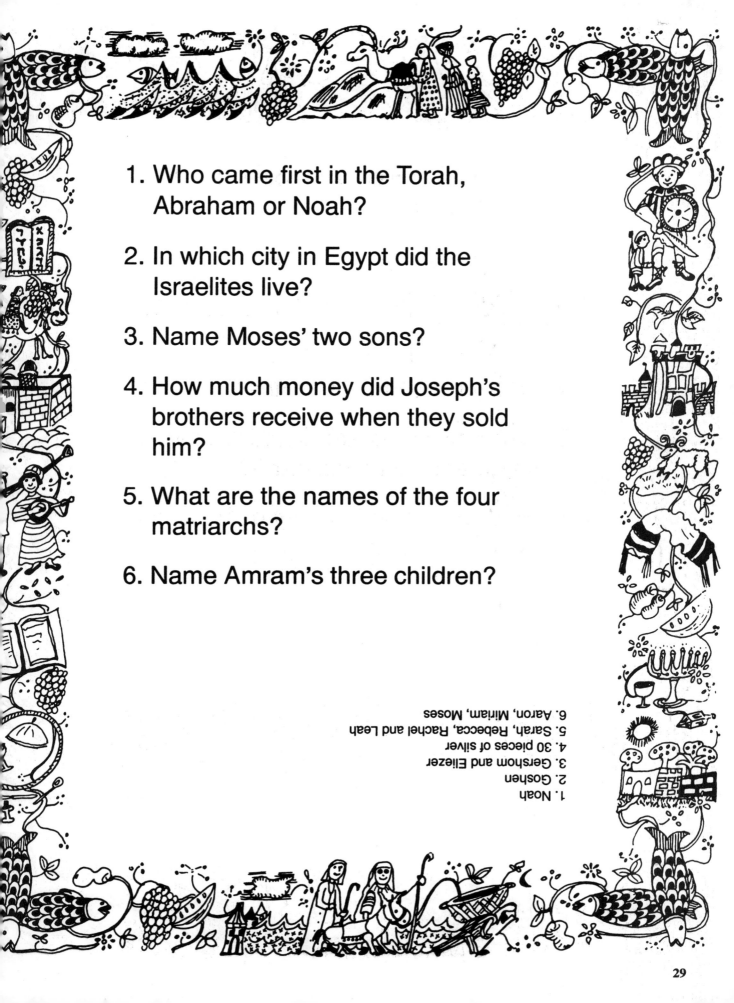

1. Who came first in the Torah, Abraham or Noah?

2. In which city in Egypt did the Israelites live?

3. Name Moses' two sons?

4. How much money did Joseph's brothers receive when they sold him?

5. What are the names of the four matriarchs?

6. Name Amram's three children?

6. Aaron, Miriam, Moses
5. Sarah, Rebecca, Rachel and Leah
4. 30 pieces of silver
3. Gershom and Eliezer
2. Goshen
1. Noah

1. Who was Jacob's only daughter?

2. Who were the parents of Moses?

3. What king threw Daniel into the lion's den?

4. What guided the Children of Israel through the desert by day?

5. What is the first commandment of the Torah?

6. What name did Pharaoh give to Joseph?

1. Dinah
2. Amram and Yocheved
3. Nebuchadnezzar
4. A pillar of cloud
5. Be fruitful and multiply
6. Tzafnat Paneach

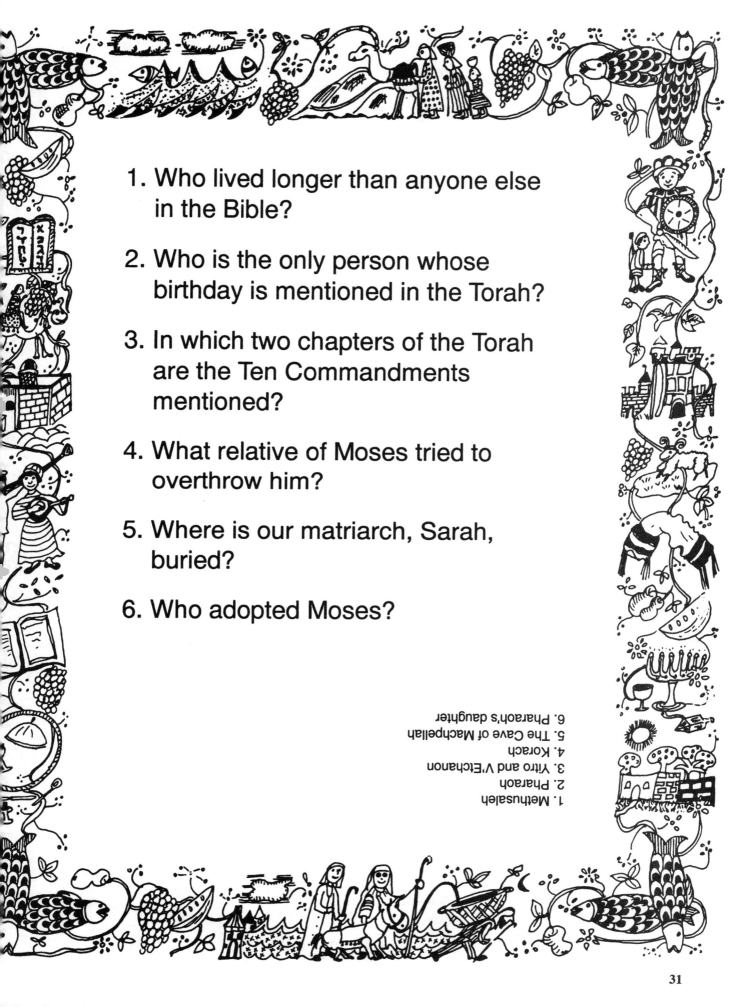

1. Who lived longer than anyone else in the Bible?

2. Who is the only person whose birthday is mentioned in the Torah?

3. In which two chapters of the Torah are the Ten Commandments mentioned?

4. What relative of Moses tried to overthrow him?

5. Where is our matriarch, Sarah, buried?

6. Who adopted Moses?

1. Methuselah
2. Pharaoh
3. Yitro and V'Etchanon
4. Korach
5. The Cave of Machpellah
6. Pharaoh's daughter

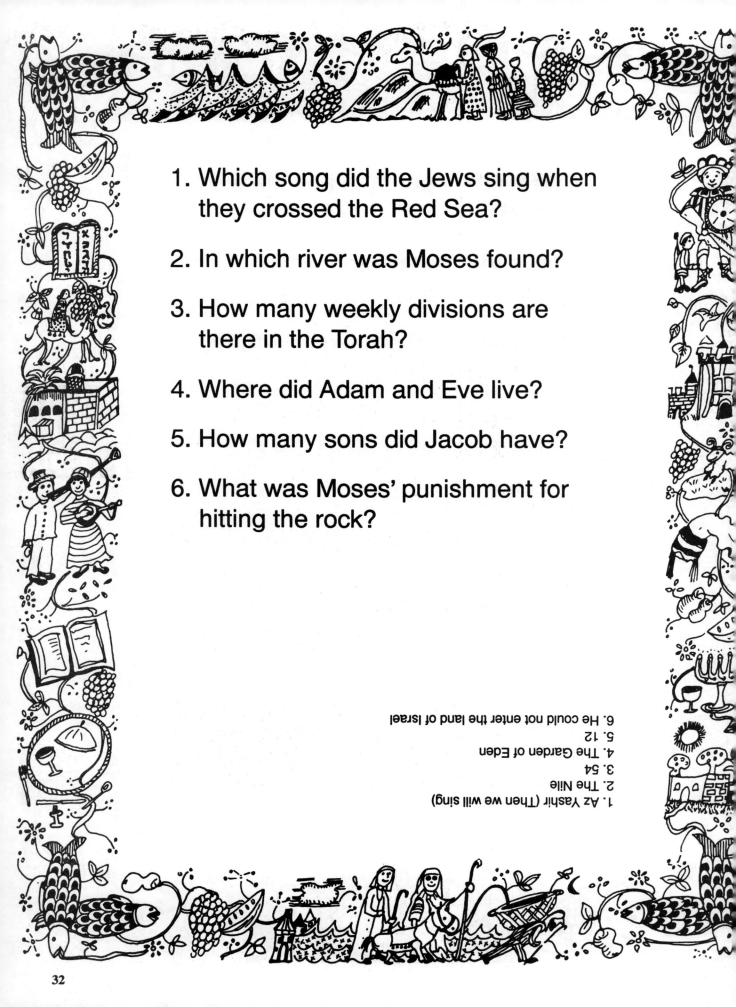

1. Which song did the Jews sing when they crossed the Red Sea?

2. In which river was Moses found?

3. How many weekly divisions are there in the Torah?

4. Where did Adam and Eve live?

5. How many sons did Jacob have?

6. What was Moses' punishment for hitting the rock?

1. Az Yashir (Then we will sing)
2. The Nile
3. 54
4. The Garden of Eden
5. 12
6. He could not enter the land of Israel

1. Name each of the five Megillot?

2. How did Haman decide the fate of the Jews?

3. Who said: "Thy people shall be my people, Thy God my God"?

4. How many years did Adam live?

5. Abraham sacrificed which animal instead of Isaac?

6. For how many years were the Jews actually slaves in Egypt?

1. Esther, Song of Songs, Ruth, Lamentations, Ecclesiastes
2. By lottery
3. Ruth to Naomi
4. 930 years
5. A ram
6. 210

1. Who was the first king of Israel?

2. Who built the First Temple?

3. A shofar blast helped cause the walls of which city to fall?

4. How old was Moses when he died?

5. Who killed Cain?

6. Who was saved from the destruction from Jericho?

Jewish Holidays

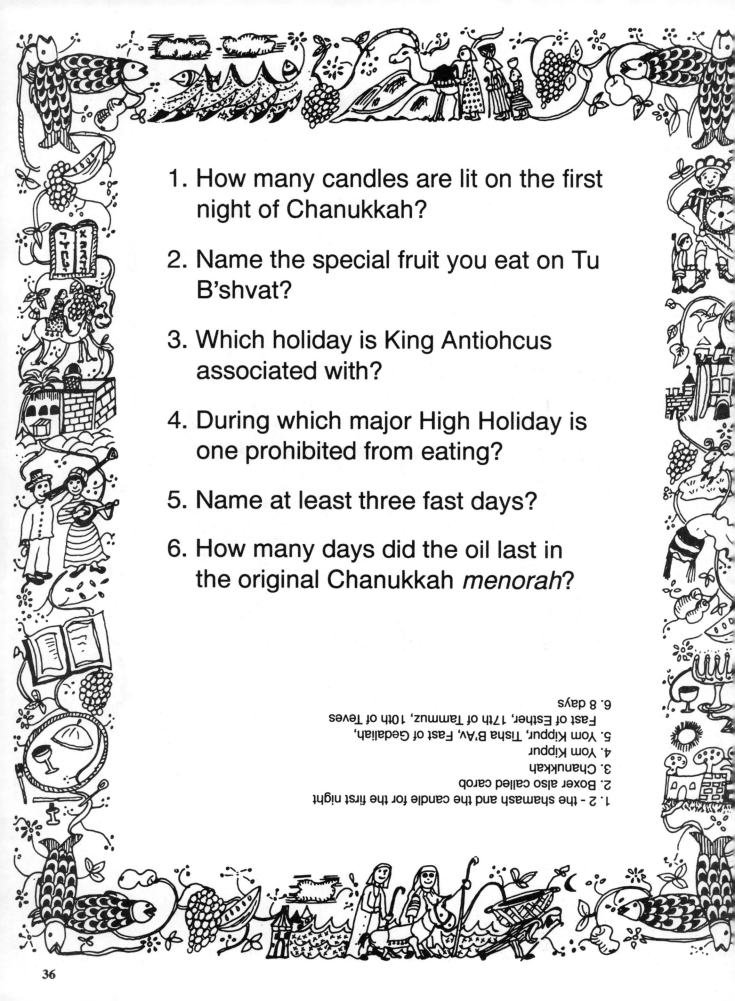

1. How many candles are lit on the first night of Chanukkah?

2. Name the special fruit you eat on Tu B'shvat?

3. Which holiday is King Antiohcus associated with?

4. During which major High Holiday is one prohibited from eating?

5. Name at least three fast days?

6. How many days did the oil last in the original Chanukkah *menorah*?

1. 2 - the shamash and the candle for the first night
2. Boxer also called carob
3. Chanukkah
4. Yom Kippur
5. Yom Kippur, Tisha B'Av, Fast of Gedaliah, Fast of Esther, 17th of Tammuz, 10th of Teves
6. 8 days

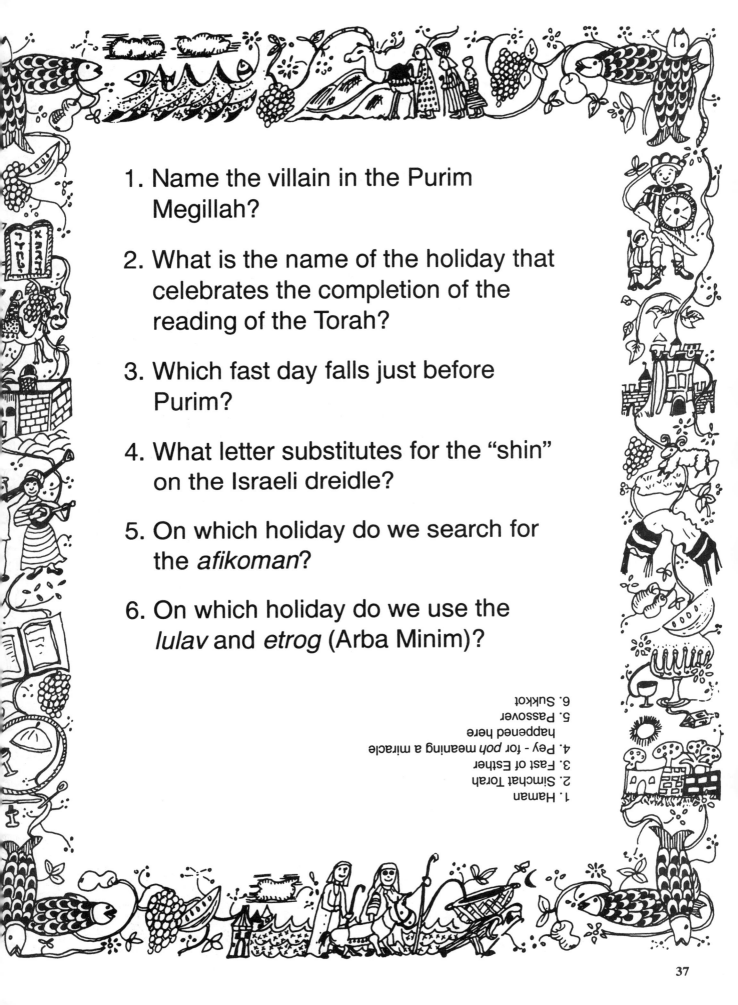

1. Name the villain in the Purim Megillah?

2. What is the name of the holiday that celebrates the completion of the reading of the Torah?

3. Which fast day falls just before Purim?

4. What letter substitutes for the "shin" on the Israeli dreidle?

5. On which holiday do we search for the *afikoman*?

6. On which holiday do we use the *lulav* and *etrog* (Arba Minim)?

1. Haman
2. Simchat Torah
3. Fast of Esther
4. Pey - for *poh* meaning a miracle happened here
5. Passover
6. Sukkot

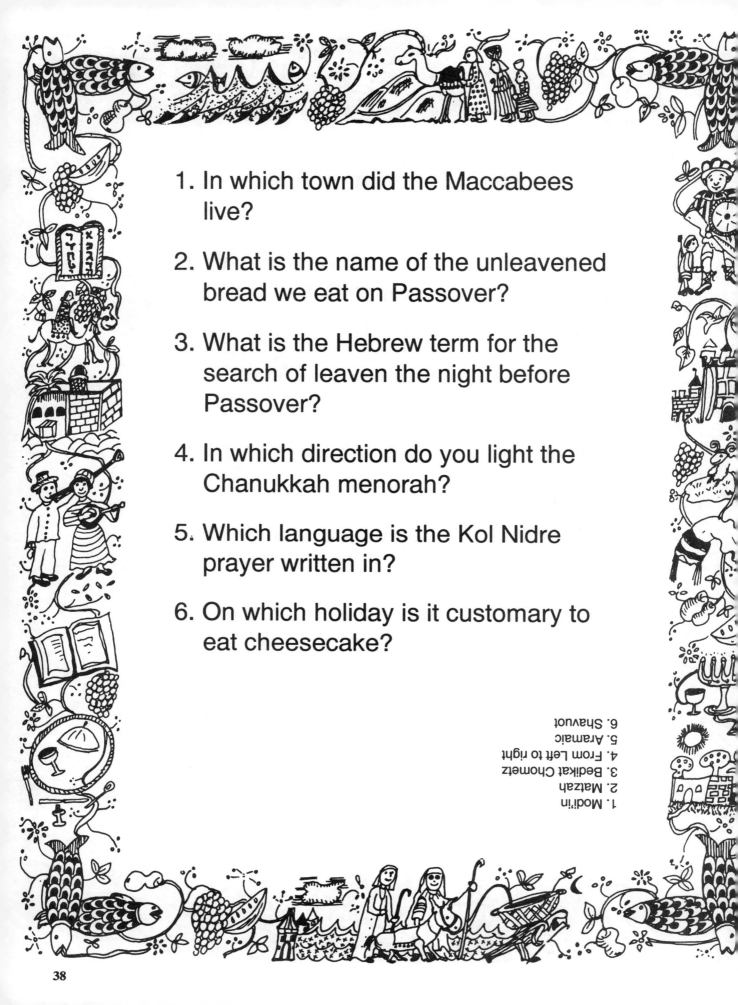

1. In which town did the Maccabees live?

2. What is the name of the unleavened bread we eat on Passover?

3. What is the Hebrew term for the search of leaven the night before Passover?

4. In which direction do you light the Chanukkah menorah?

5. Which language is the Kol Nidre prayer written in?

6. On which holiday is it customary to eat cheesecake?

1. Modi'in
2. Matzah
3. Bedikat Chometz
4. From Left to right
5. Aramaic
6. Shavuot

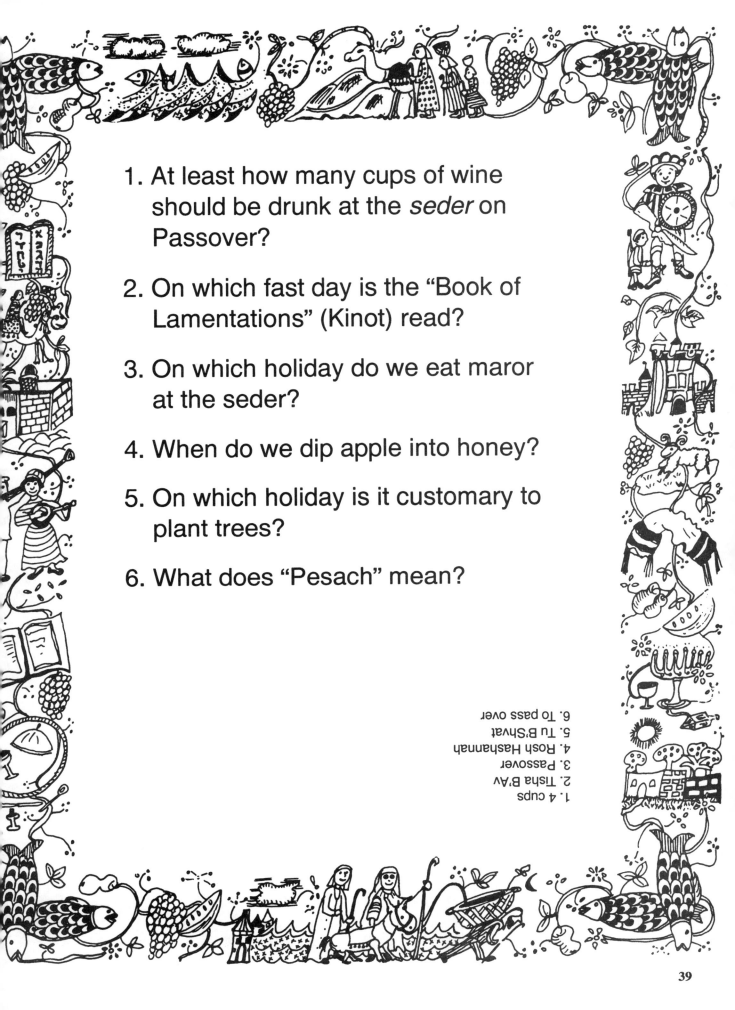

1. At least how many cups of wine should be drunk at the *seder* on Passover?

2. On which fast day is the "Book of Lamentations" (Kinot) read?

3. On which holiday do we eat maror at the seder?

4. When do we dip apple into honey?

5. On which holiday is it customary to plant trees?

6. What does "Pesach" mean?

1. 4 cups
2. Tisha B'Av
3. Passover
4. Rosh Hashannah
5. Tu B'Shvat
6. To pass over

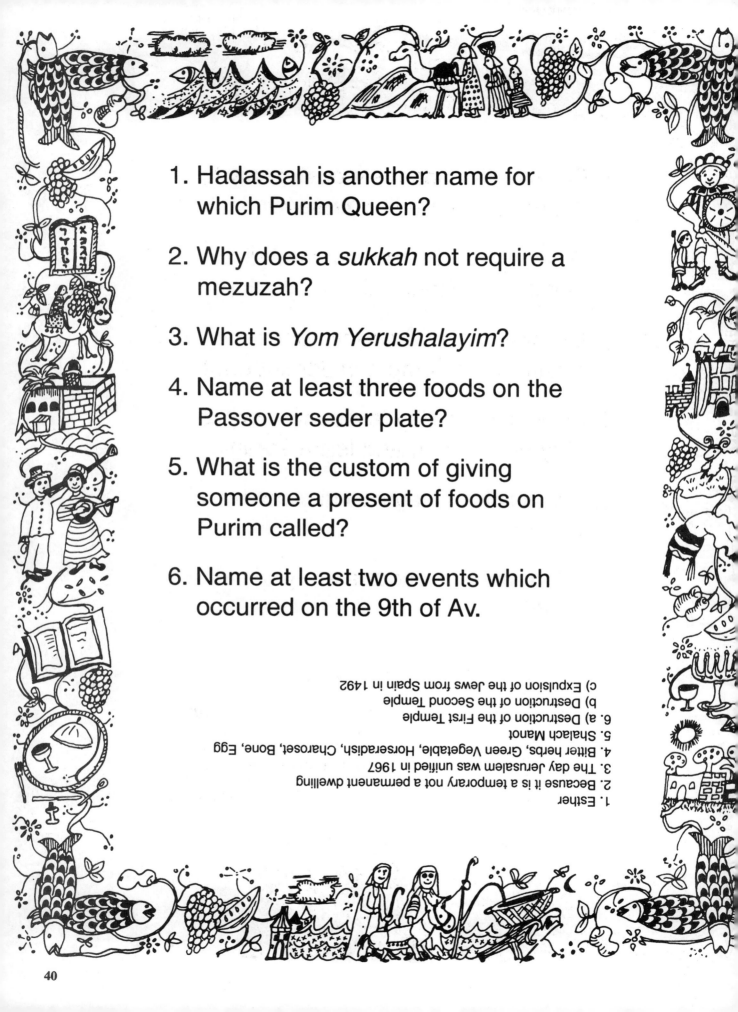

1. Hadassah is another name for which Purim Queen?

2. Why does a *sukkah* not require a mezuzah?

3. What is *Yom Yerushalayim*?

4. Name at least three foods on the Passover seder plate?

5. What is the custom of giving someone a present of foods on Purim called?

6. Name at least two events which occurred on the 9th of Av.

1. Esther
2. Because it is a temporary not a permanent dwelling
3. The day Jerusalem was unified in 1967
4. Bitter herbs, Green Vegetable, Horseradish, Charoset, Bone, Egg
5. Shalach Manot
6. a) Destruction of the First Temple
   b) Destruction of the Second Temple
   c) Expulsion of the Jews from Spain in 1492

1. On which holiday is it customary for the child to recite the "Ma Nishtanah?"

2. What is the Hebrew date on which Chanukkah begins?

3. On which three holidays did Jews travel to the Temple in Jerusalem?

4. On which holiday is it customary to stay up all night and learn Torah?

5. On which holiday do we read the Book of Ruth?

6. When do we read the story of Jonah?

1. Passover
2. 25th of Kislev
3. Passover, Sukkot, and Shavuot
4. Shavuot
5. Shavuot
6. Yom Kippur

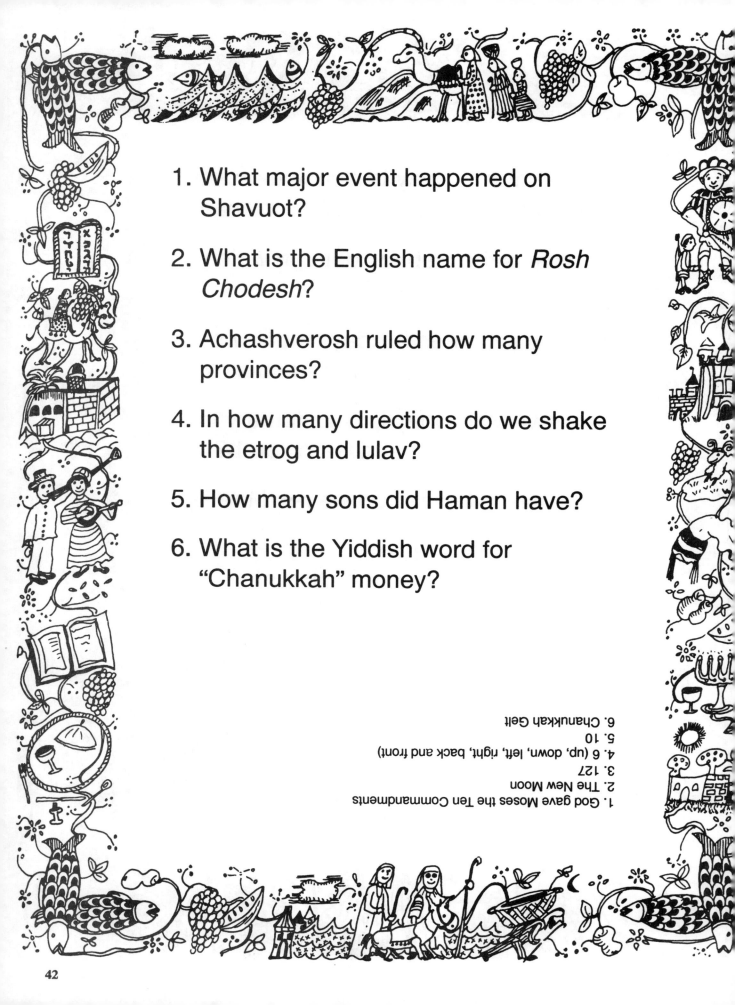

1. What major event happened on Shavuot?

2. What is the English name for *Rosh Chodesh*?

3. Achashverosh ruled how many provinces?

4. In how many directions do we shake the etrog and lulav?

5. How many sons did Haman have?

6. What is the Yiddish word for "Chanukkah" money?

1. God gave Moses the Ten Commandments
2. The New Moon
3. 127
4. 6 (up, down, left, right, back and front)
5. 10
6. Chanukkah Gelt

1. How many *matzahs* are covered at the seder table?

2. How many sons are mentioned in the Hagaddah?

3. On what holiday do all the young children come up to get an *aliyah* (blessing at the Torah)?

4. What is the name given to the last day of Sukkot?

5. What is another name for the Greeks of the Maccabee period?

6. How many times is the Megillah (Book of Esther) read on Purim?

1. 3
2. 4
3. Simchat Torah
4. Hoshannah Rabbah
5. Hellenists
6. Twice

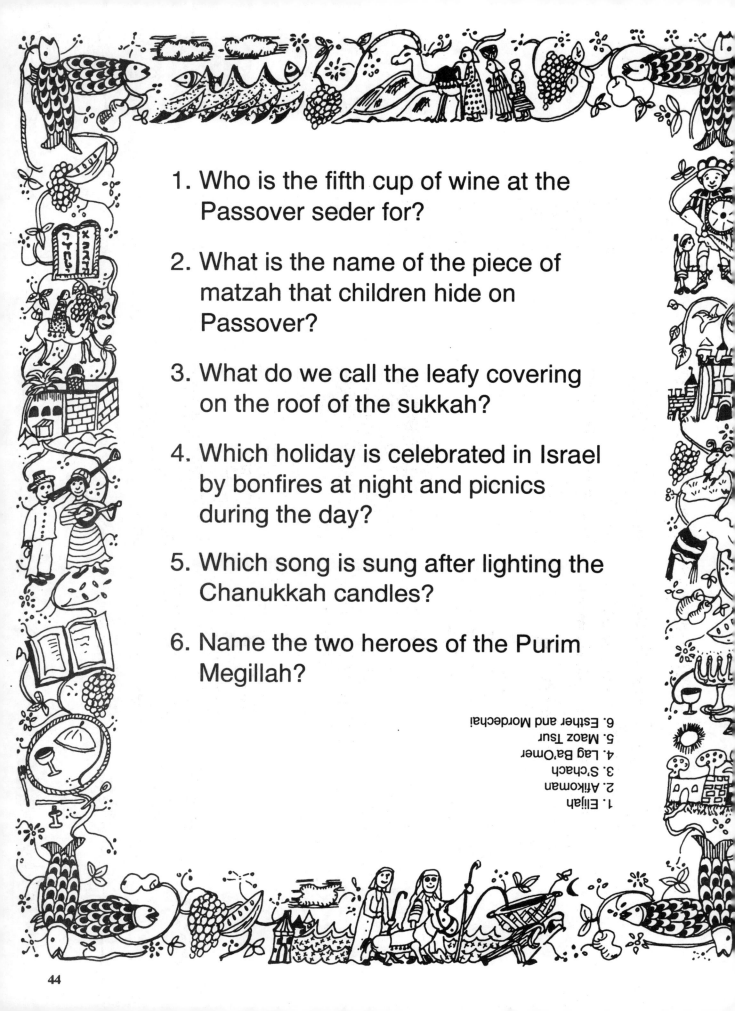

1. Who is the fifth cup of wine at the Passover seder for?

2. What is the name of the piece of matzah that children hide on Passover?

3. What do we call the leafy covering on the roof of the sukkah?

4. Which holiday is celebrated in Israel by bonfires at night and picnics during the day?

5. Which song is sung after lighting the Chanukkah candles?

6. Name the two heroes of the Purim Megillah?

1. Elijah
2. Afikoman
3. S'chach
4. Lag Ba'Omer
5. Maoz Tsur
6. Esther and Mordechai

Arts and Literature

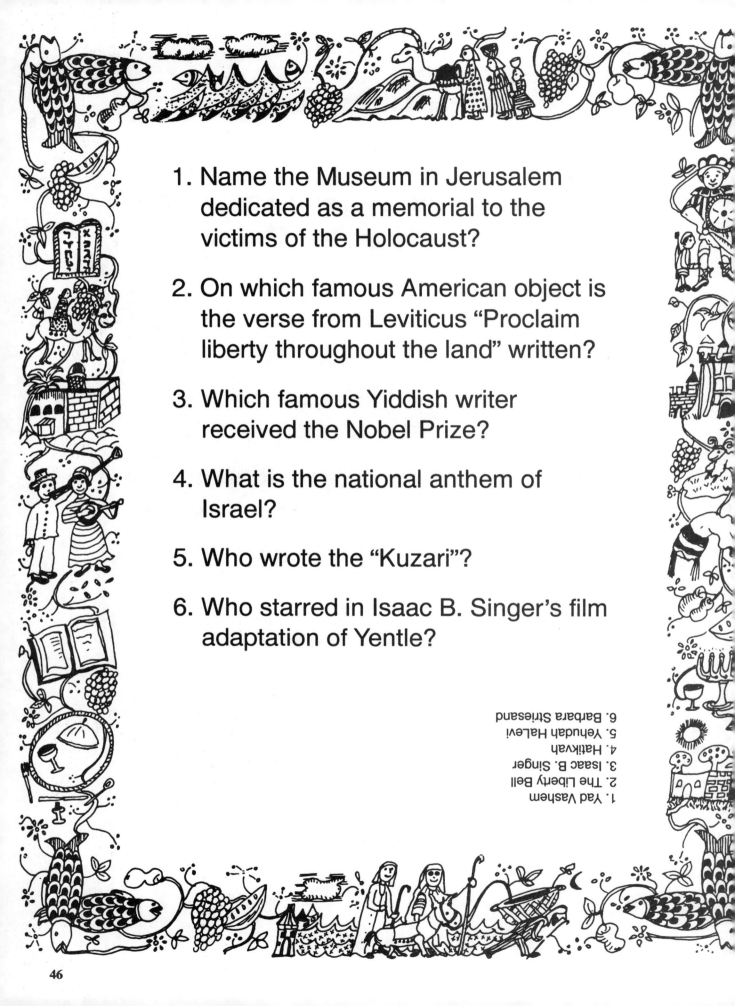

1. Name the Museum in Jerusalem dedicated as a memorial to the victims of the Holocaust?

2. On which famous American object is the verse from Leviticus "Proclaim liberty throughout the land" written?

3. Which famous Yiddish writer received the Nobel Prize?

4. What is the national anthem of Israel?

5. Who wrote the "Kuzari"?

6. Who starred in Isaac B. Singer's film adaptation of Yentle?

1. Yad Vashem
2. The Liberty Bell
3. Isaac B. Singer
4. Hatikvah
5. Yehudah Halevi
6. Barbara Striesand

1. Who wrote "The Chosen?"

2. Who was the most famous commentator of the Torah?

3. What was Tevye's profession in "Fiddler on the Roof"?

4. Who is the first Israeli to win the Nobel Prize in Literature?

5. Who founded the Bezalel school of art in Israel?

6. Which Israeli poet is known as the greatest Hebrew poet in modern times?

1. Chaim Potok
2. Rashi
3. Milkman
4. S.Y. Agnon
5. Boris Shatz
6. Hayyim Nachman Bialik

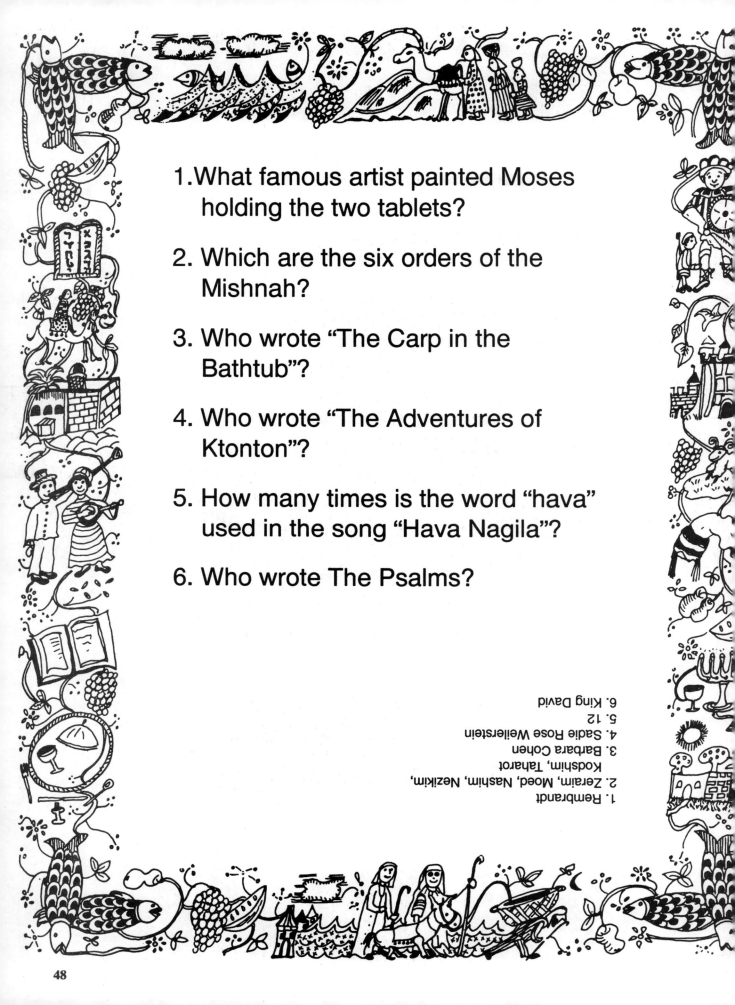

1. What famous artist painted Moses holding the two tablets?

2. Which are the six orders of the Mishnah?

3. Who wrote "The Carp in the Bathtub"?

4. Who wrote "The Adventures of Ktonton"?

5. How many times is the word "hava" used in the song "Hava Nagila"?

6. Who wrote The Psalms?

1. Rembrandt
2. Zeraim, Moed, Nashim, Nezikim, Kodshim, Taharot
3. Barbara Cohen
4. Sadie Rose Weilerstein
5. 12
6. King David

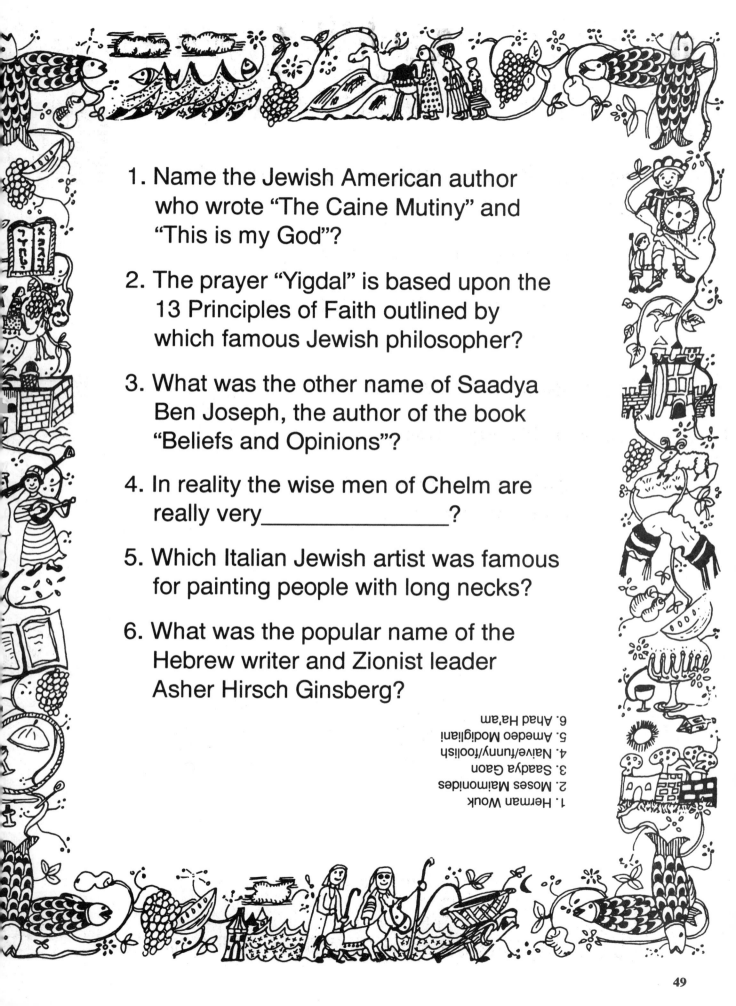

1. Name the Jewish American author who wrote "The Caine Mutiny" and "This is my God"?

2. The prayer "Yigdal" is based upon the 13 Principles of Faith outlined by which famous Jewish philosopher?

3. What was the other name of Saadya Ben Joseph, the author of the book "Beliefs and Opinions"?

4. In reality the wise men of Chelm are really very_____?

5. Which Italian Jewish artist was famous for painting people with long necks?

6. What was the popular name of the Hebrew writer and Zionist leader Asher Hirsch Ginsberg?

1. Herman Wouk
2. Moses Maimonides
3. Saadya Gaon
4. Naive/funny/foolish
5. Amedeo Modigliani
6. Ahad Ha'am

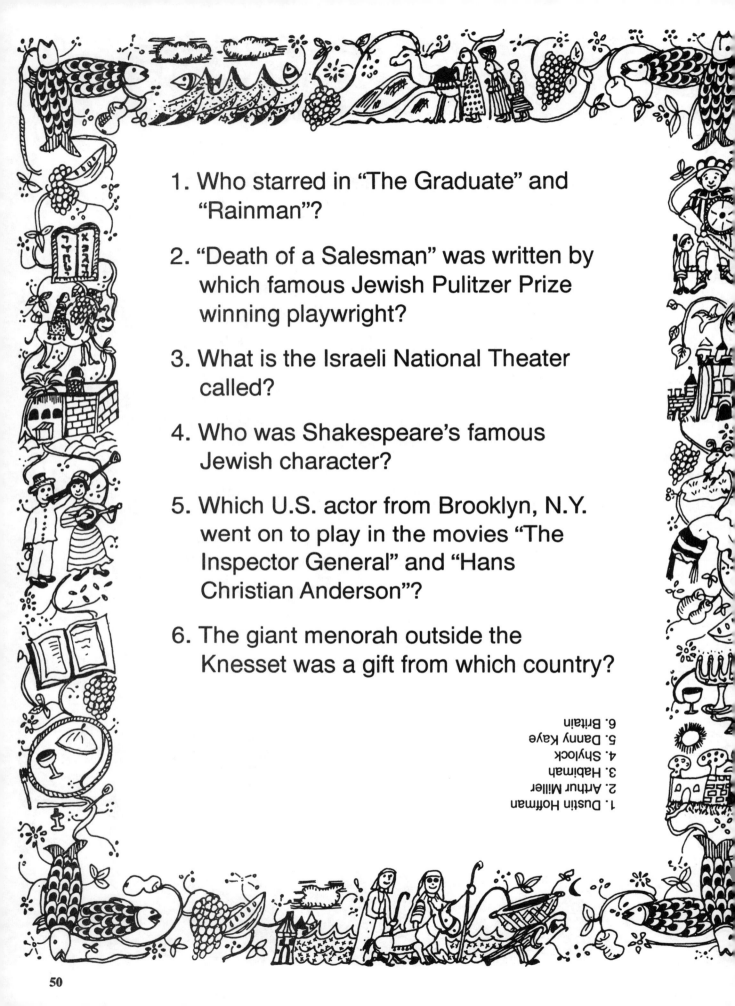

1. Who starred in "The Graduate" and "Rainman"?

2. "Death of a Salesman" was written by which famous Jewish Pulitzer Prize winning playwright?

3. What is the Israeli National Theater called?

4. Who was Shakespeare's famous Jewish character?

5. Which U.S. actor from Brooklyn, N.Y. went on to play in the movies "The Inspector General" and "Hans Christian Anderson"?

6. The giant menorah outside the Knesset was a gift from which country?

1. Dustin Hoffman
2. Arthur Miller
3. Habimah
4. Shylock
5. Danny Kaye
6. Britain

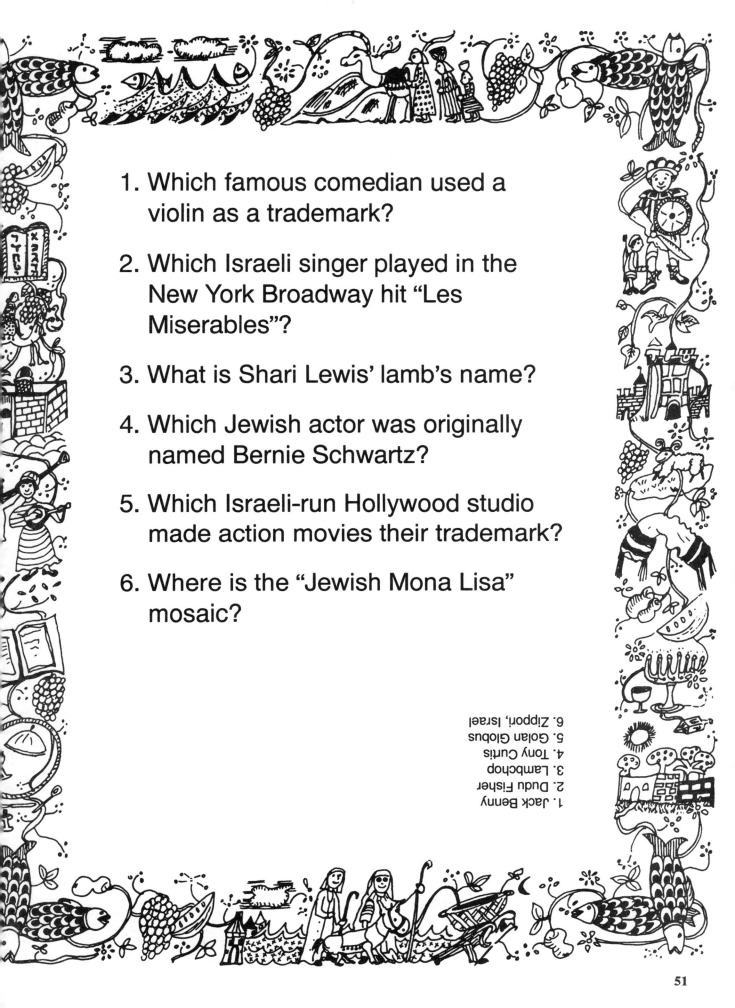

1. Which famous comedian used a violin as a trademark?

2. Which Israeli singer played in the New York Broadway hit "Les Miserables"?

3. What is Shari Lewis' lamb's name?

4. Which Jewish actor was originally named Bernie Schwartz?

5. Which Israeli-run Hollywood studio made action movies their trademark?

6. Where is the "Jewish Mona Lisa" mosaic?

1. Jack Benny
2. Dudu Fisher
3. Lambchop
4. Tony Curtis
5. Golan Globus
6. Zippori, Israel

1. Which 2 Jewish singers starred in the two versions of "The Jazz Singer"?

2. Which Jewish actor starred in "Spartacus"?

3. Who wrote the novel "Exodus"?

4. Which Sabbath dish is affectionately called "Jewish Soul Food"?

5. This language of European Jewry was comprised mainly of German and Hebrew.

6. Which Israeli is famous for bending spoons?

1. Al Jolson and Neil Diamond
2. Kirk Douglas
3. Leon Uris
4. Cholent
5. Yiddish
6. Uri Geller

1. Which movie producer made a film of the life of Oskar Schindler?

2. Who was the Bible's finest artisan?

3. Who sang and composed the song "Jerusalem The Golden?"

4. Who was the "Singing Rabbi" that helped popularize modern Jewish music?

5. Who wrote the "All-of-a-kind" family series?

6. Who was the editor of the Mishnah?

1. Steven Spielberg with the movie "Schindler's List"
2. Bezalel
3. Naomi Shemer
4. Shlomo Carlebach
5. Sydney Taylor
6. Judah Ha-Nasi

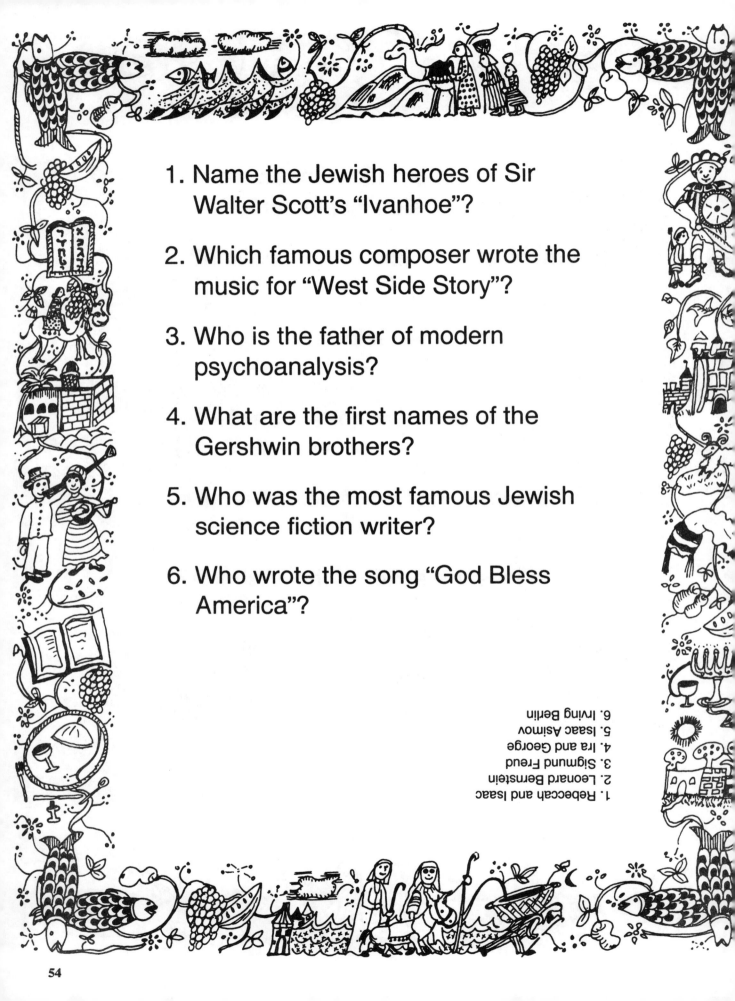

1. Name the Jewish heroes of Sir Walter Scott's "Ivanhoe"?

2. Which famous composer wrote the music for "West Side Story"?

3. Who is the father of modern psychoanalysis?

4. What are the first names of the Gershwin brothers?

5. Who was the most famous Jewish science fiction writer?

6. Who wrote the song "God Bless America"?

1. Rebeccah and Isaac
2. Leonard Bernstein
3. Sigmund Freud
4. Ira and George
5. Isaac Asimov
6. Irving Berlin

Customs and Laws

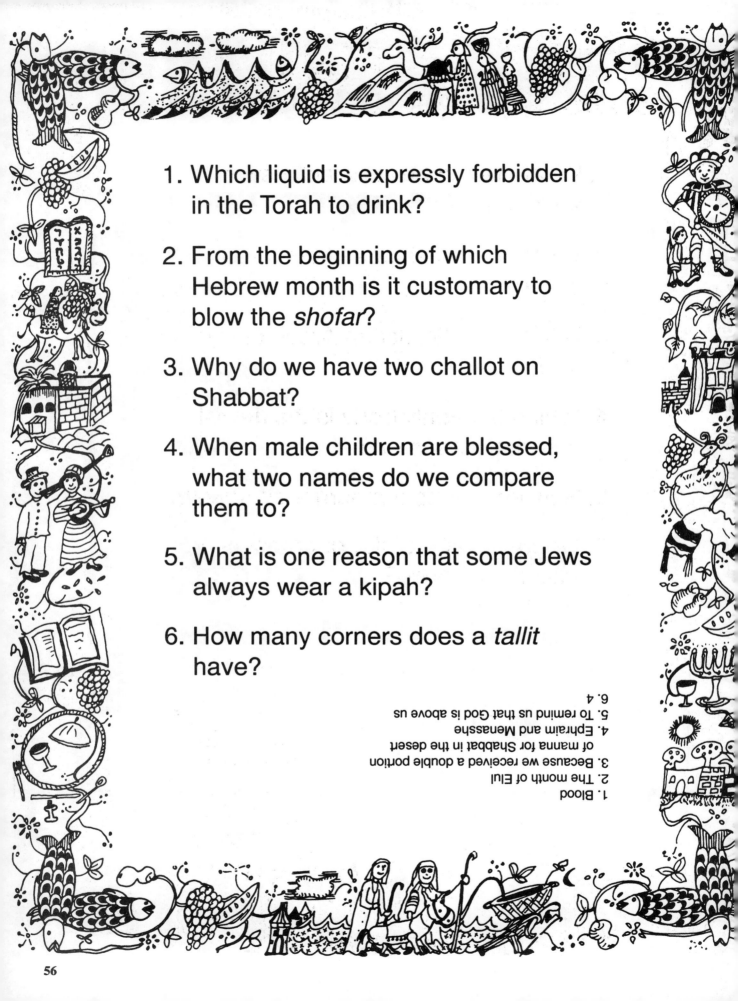

1. Which liquid is expressly forbidden in the Torah to drink?

2. From the beginning of which Hebrew month is it customary to blow the *shofar*?

3. Why do we have two challot on Shabbat?

4. When male children are blessed, what two names do we compare them to?

5. What is one reason that some Jews always wear a kipah?

6. How many corners does a *tallit* have?

1. Blood
2. The month of Elul
3. Because we received a double portion of manna for Shabbat in the desert
4. Ephraim and Menasshe
5. To remind us that God is above us
6. 4

1. What are the two characteristics of kosher fish?

2. What are the fringes of the tallit called?

3. What is the Shulchan Aruch called in English?

4. Which heavenly body is the Jewish calendar based on?

5. How long does a mourner sit *shivah*?

6. On which side of the doorpost is the mezuzah placed?

1. Fins and scales
2. Tzitzit
3. Code of Jewish Law
4. The moon
5. 7 days
6. Right

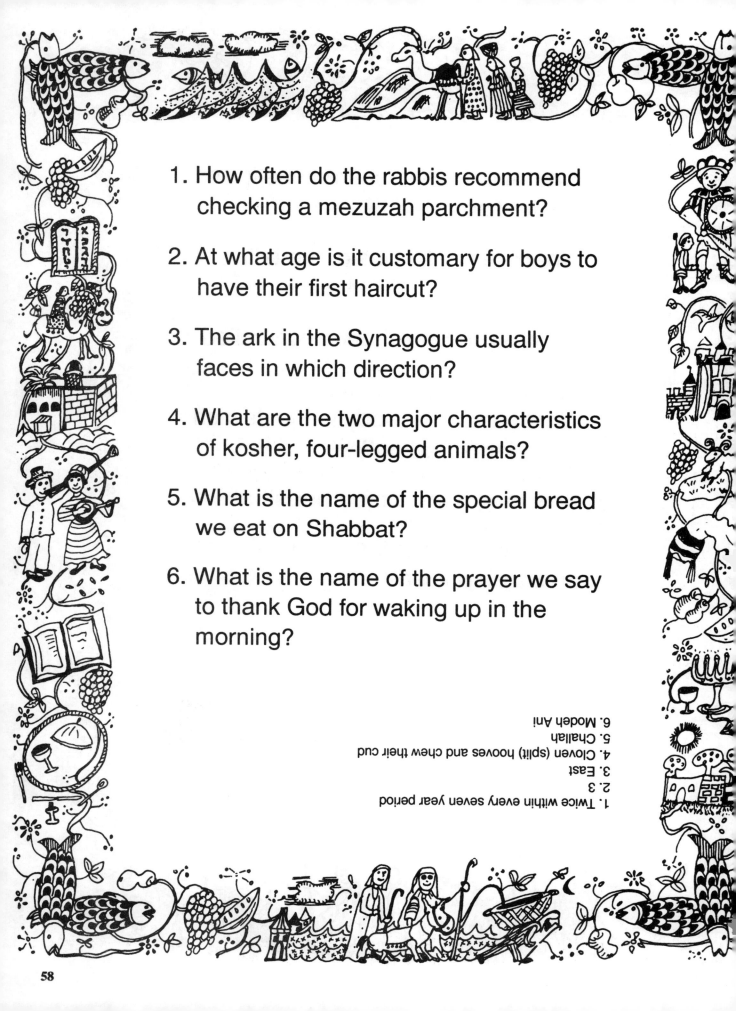

1. How often do the rabbis recommend checking a mezuzah parchment?

2. At what age is it customary for boys to have their first haircut?

3. The ark in the Synagogue usually faces in which direction?

4. What are the two major characteristics of kosher, four-legged animals?

5. What is the name of the special bread we eat on Shabbat?

6. What is the name of the prayer we say to thank God for waking up in the morning?

1. Twice within every seven year period
2. 3
3. East
4. Cloven (split) hooves and chew their cud
5. Challah
6. Modeh Ani

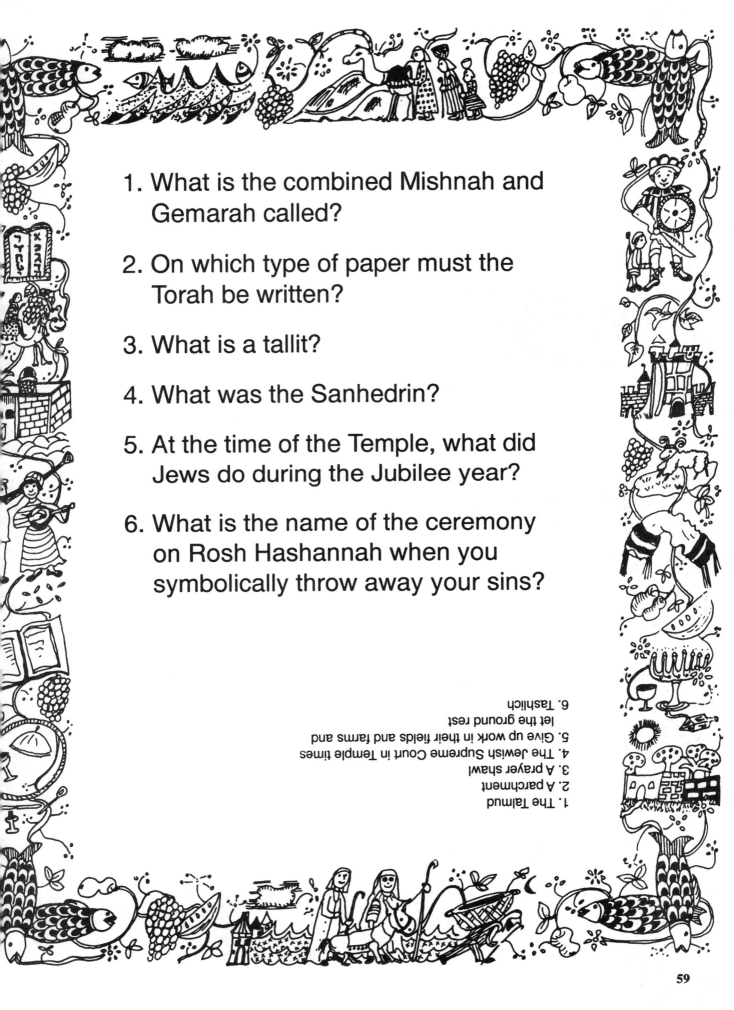

1. What is the combined Mishnah and Gemarah called?

2. On which type of paper must the Torah be written?

3. What is a tallit?

4. What was the Sanhedrin?

5. At the time of the Temple, what did Jews do during the Jubilee year?

6. What is the name of the ceremony on Rosh Hashannah when you symbolically throw away your sins?

1. The Talmud
2. A parchment
3. A prayer shawl
4. The Jewish Supreme Court in Temple times
5. Give up work in their fields and farms and let the ground rest
6. Tashlich

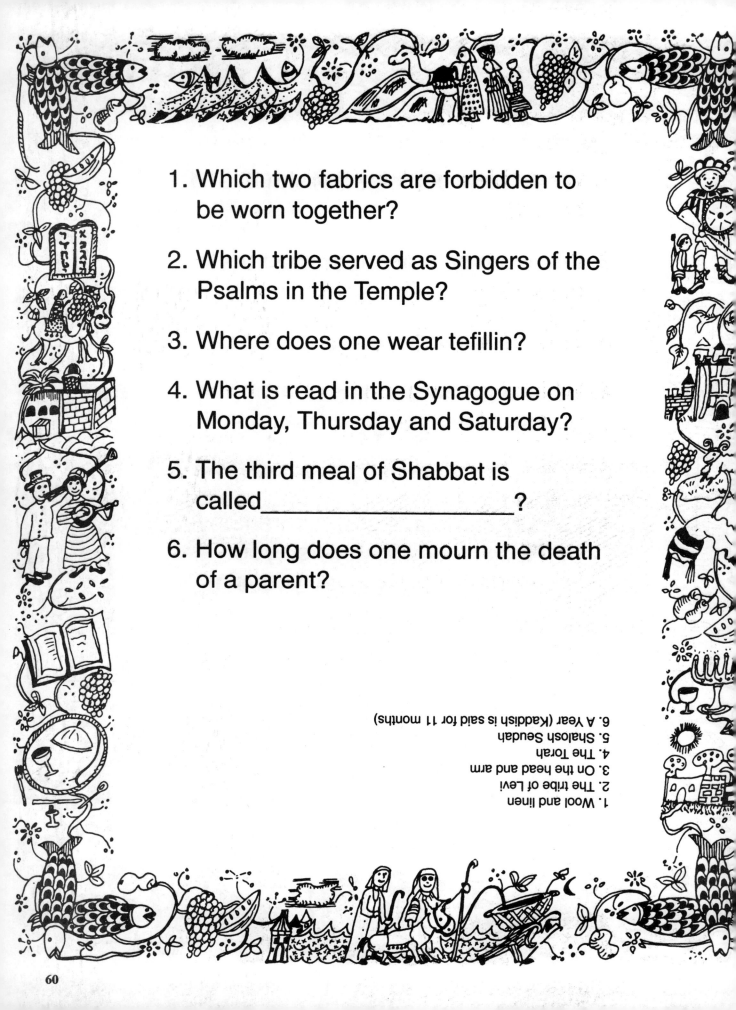

1. Which two fabrics are forbidden to be worn together?

2. Which tribe served as Singers of the Psalms in the Temple?

3. Where does one wear tefillin?

4. What is read in the Synagogue on Monday, Thursday and Saturday?

5. The third meal of Shabbat is called_____?

6. How long does one mourn the death of a parent?

1. Wool and linen
2. The tribe of Levi
3. On the head and arm
4. The Torah
5. Shalosh Seudah
6. A Year (Kaddish is said for 11 months)

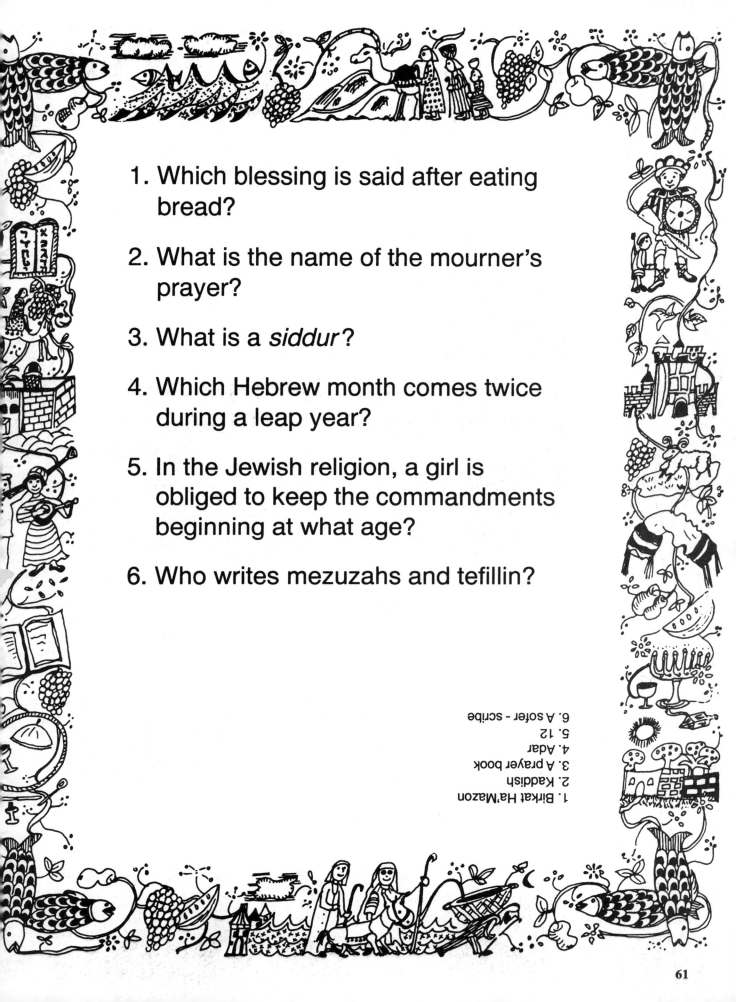

1. Which blessing is said after eating bread?

2. What is the name of the mourner's prayer?

3. What is a *siddur*?

4. Which Hebrew month comes twice during a leap year?

5. In the Jewish religion, a girl is obliged to keep the commandments beginning at what age?

6. Who writes mezuzahs and tefillin?

1. Birkat Ha'Mazon
2. Kaddish
3. A prayer book
4. Adar
5. 12
6. A sofer – scribe

1. How many days are there in a Hebrew month?

2. Which letter is on the outside of the mezuzah?

3. When does Shabbat begin?

4. Is a green etrog kosher?

5. How often does a Jewish leap year occur?

6. How many articles of clothing were worn by the Kohen Gadol in the Temple?

6. 8
5. 7 times every 19 years
4. Yes
3. On Friday afternoon at Sundown
2. Shin
1. 29 or 30

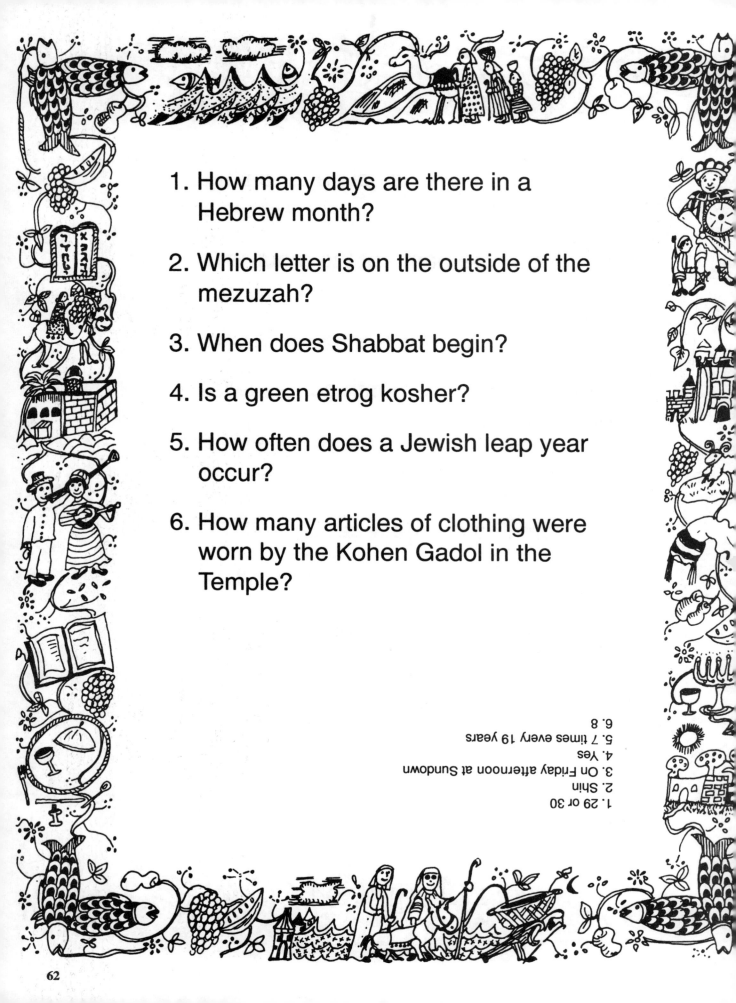

Hebrew Language

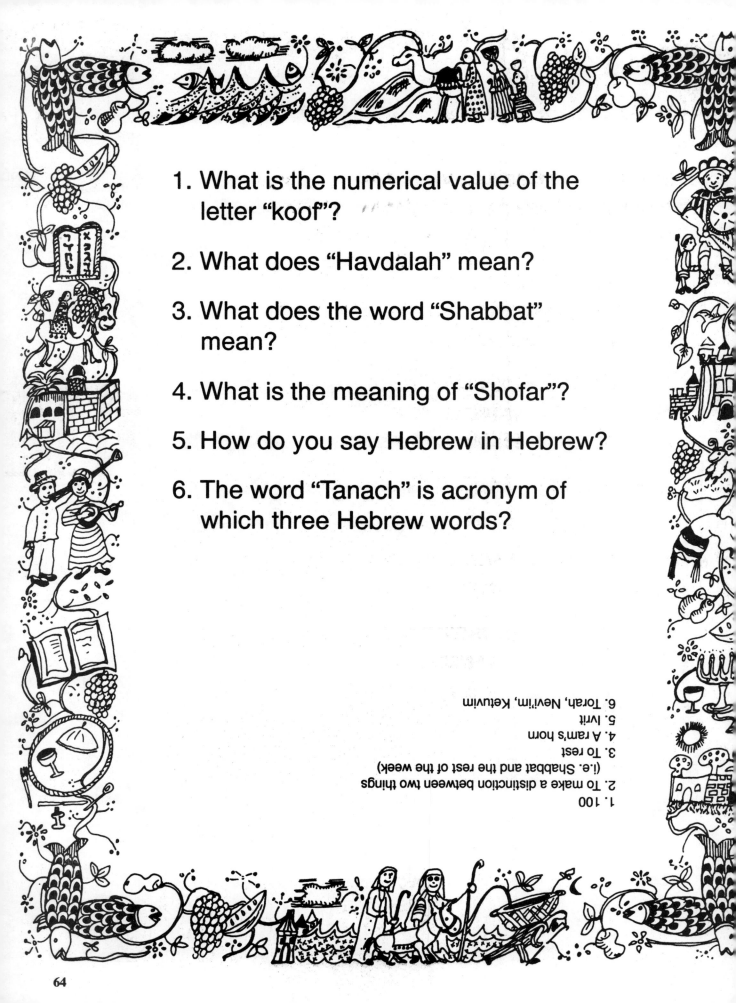

1. What is the numerical value of the letter "koof"?

2. What does "Havdalah" mean?

3. What does the word "Shabbat" mean?

4. What is the meaning of "Shofar"?

5. How do you say Hebrew in Hebrew?

6. The word "Tanach" is acronym of which three Hebrew words?

1. 100
2. To make a distinction between two things (i.e. Shabbat and the rest of the week)
3. To rest
4. A ram's horn
5. Ivrit
6. Torah, Nevi'im, Ketuvim

1. What is the Hebrew word for the Five Books of Moses?

2. What is the name given to the kosher slaughter of meat?

3. What is immigration to Israel called?

4. What does "Jaffa" mean?

5. What does "Seder" mean?

6. What is the "Galut"?

1. Chumash or Torah
2. Shechitah
3. Aliyah
4. Beautiful
5. Order
6. Exile

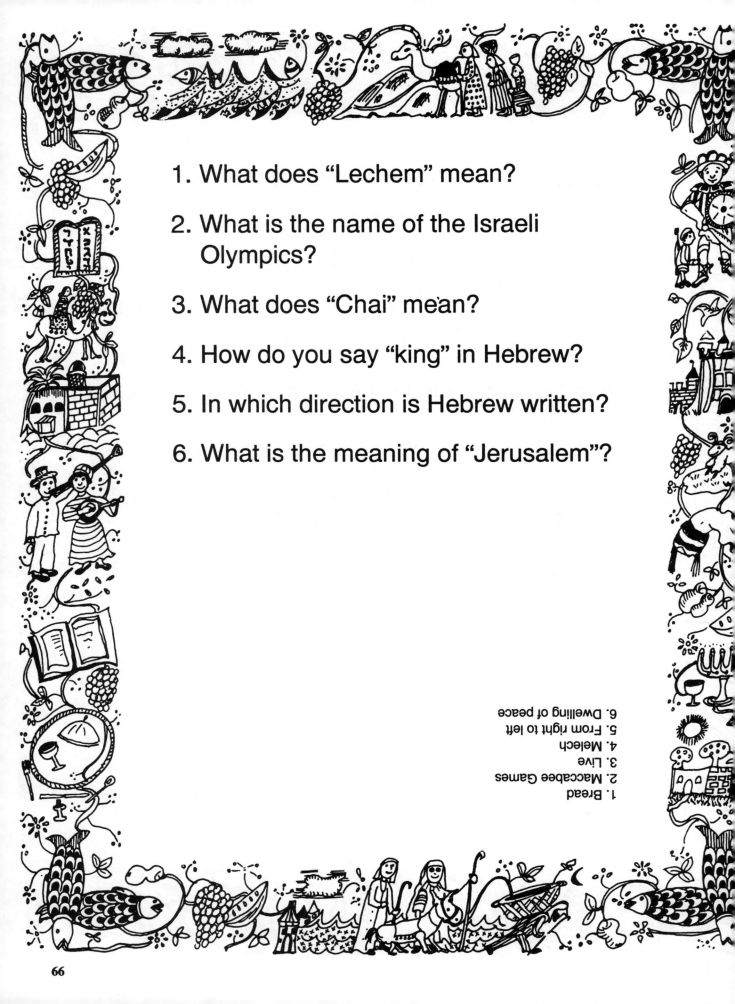

1. What does "Lechem" mean?

2. What is the name of the Israeli Olympics?

3. What does "Chai" mean?

4. How do you say "king" in Hebrew?

5. In which direction is Hebrew written?

6. What is the meaning of "Jerusalem"?

1. Bread
2. Maccabee Games
3. Live
4. Melech
5. From right to left
6. Dwelling of peace

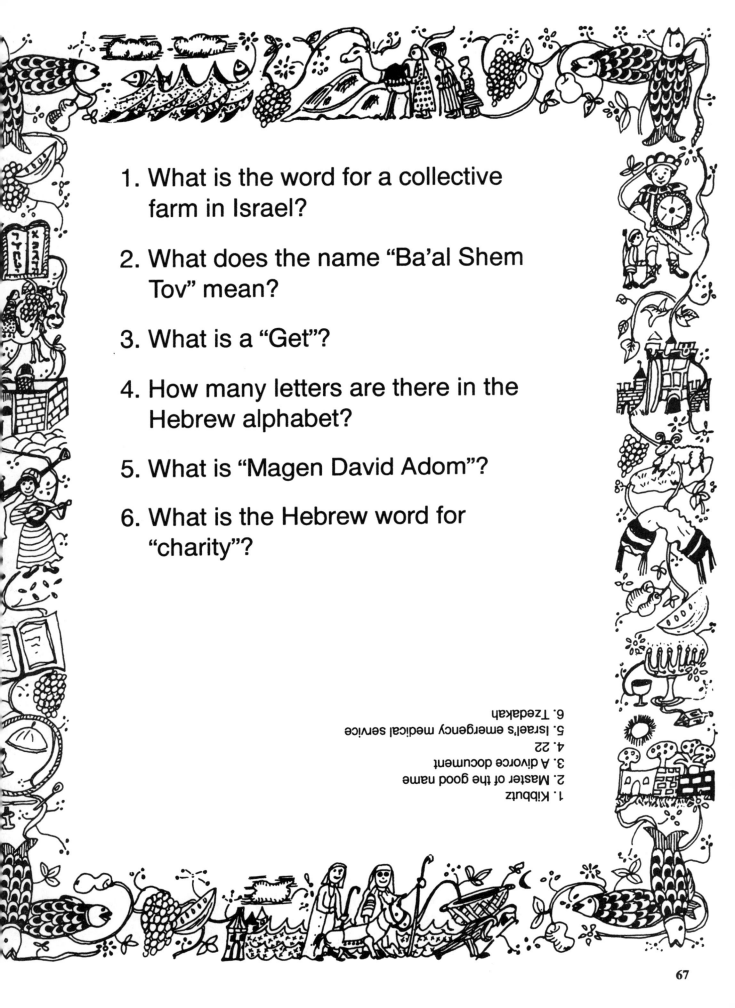

1. What is the word for a collective farm in Israel?

2. What does the name "Ba'al Shem Tov" mean?

3. What is a "Get"?

4. How many letters are there in the Hebrew alphabet?

5. What is "Magen David Adom"?

6. What is the Hebrew word for "charity"?

1. Kibbutz
2. Master of the good name
3. A divorce document
4. 22
5. Israel's emergency medical service
6. Tzedakah

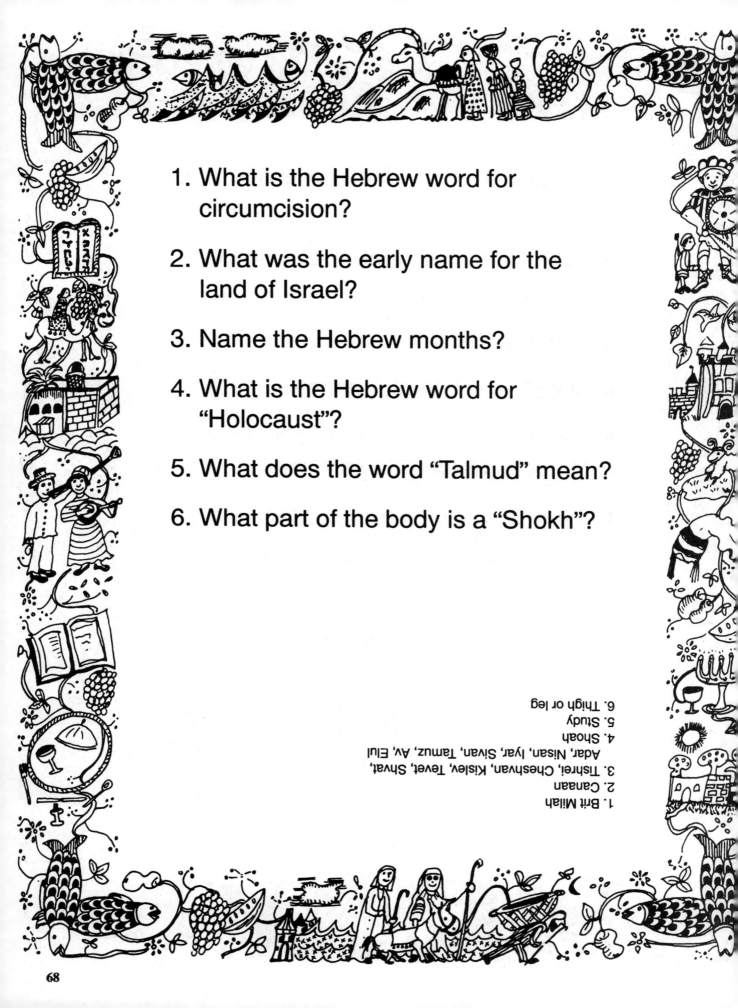

1. What is the Hebrew word for circumcision?

2. What was the early name for the land of Israel?

3. Name the Hebrew months?

4. What is the Hebrew word for "Holocaust"?

5. What does the word "Talmud" mean?

6. What part of the body is a "Shokh"?

1. Brit Milah
2. Canaan
3. Tishrei, Cheshvan, Kislev, Tevet, Shvat, Adar, Nisan, Iyar, Sivan, Tamuz, Av, Elul
4. Shoah
5. Study
6. Thigh or leg

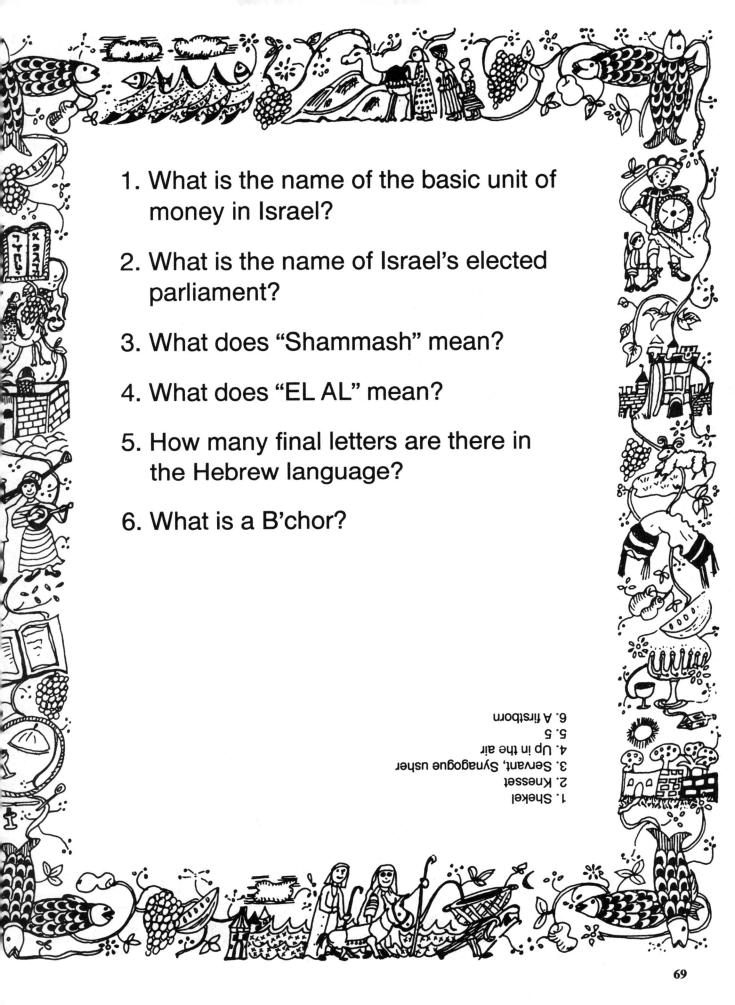

1. What is the name of the basic unit of money in Israel?

2. What is the name of Israel's elected parliament?

3. What does "Shammash" mean?

4. What does "EL AL" mean?

5. How many final letters are there in the Hebrew language?

6. What is a B'chor?

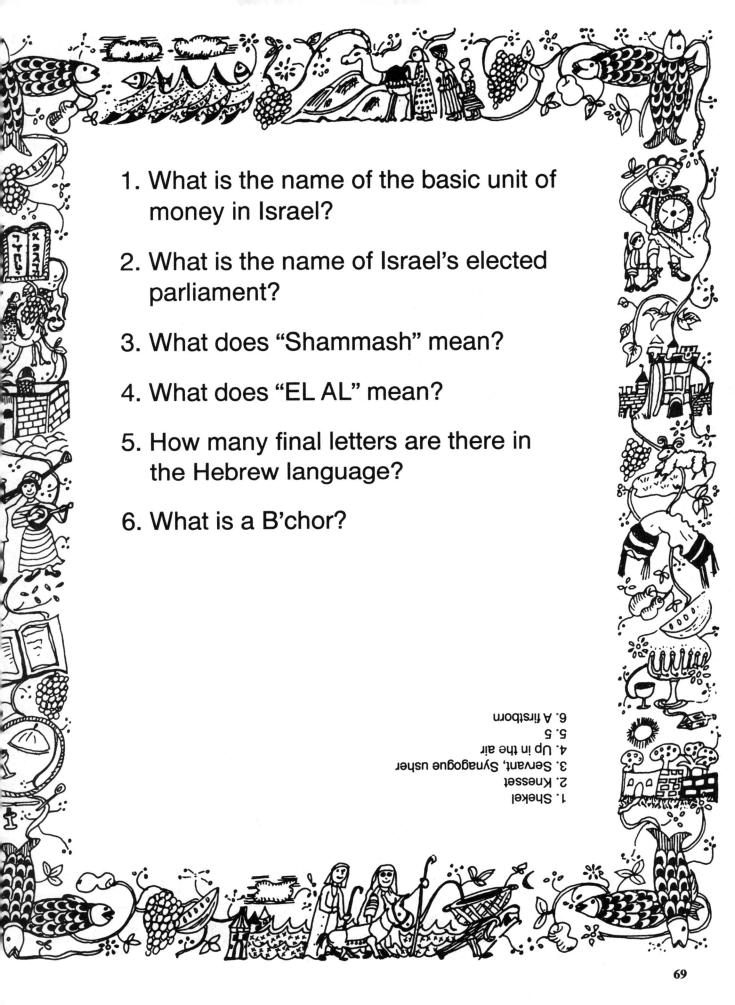

1. Shekel
2. Knesset
3. Servant, Synagogue usher
4. Up in the air
5. 5
6. A firstborn

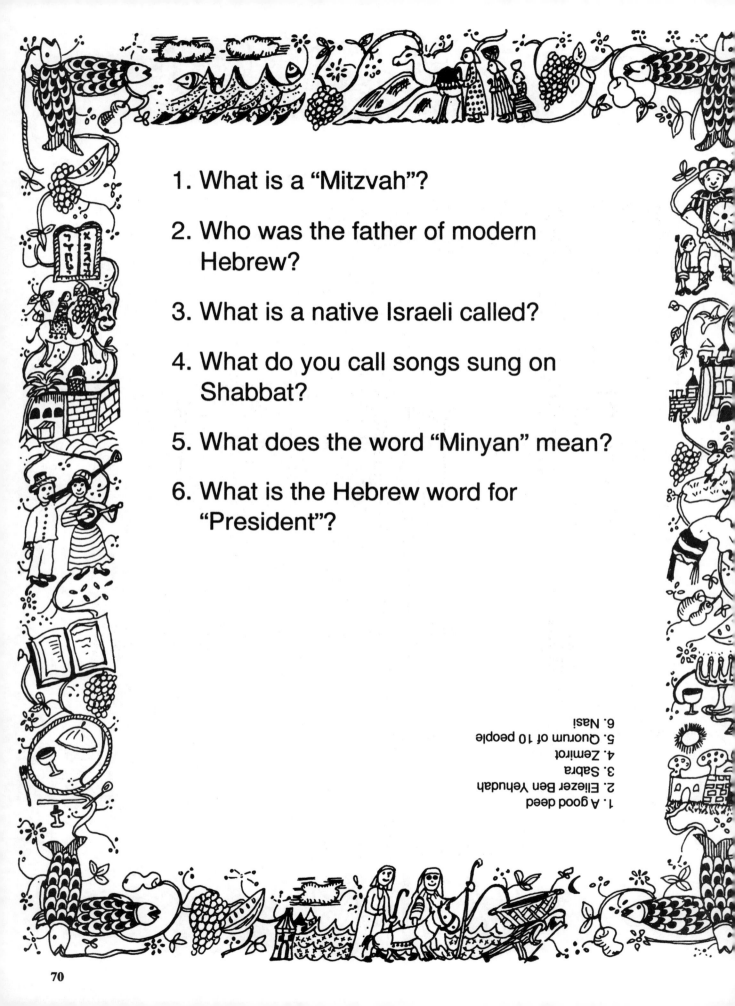

1. What is a "Mitzvah"?

2. Who was the father of modern Hebrew?

3. What is a native Israeli called?

4. What do you call songs sung on Shabbat?

5. What does the word "Minyan" mean?

6. What is the Hebrew word for "President"?

1. A good deed
2. Eliezer Ben Yehudah
3. Sabra
4. Zemirot
5. Quorum of 10 people
6. Nasi

Jewish Geography

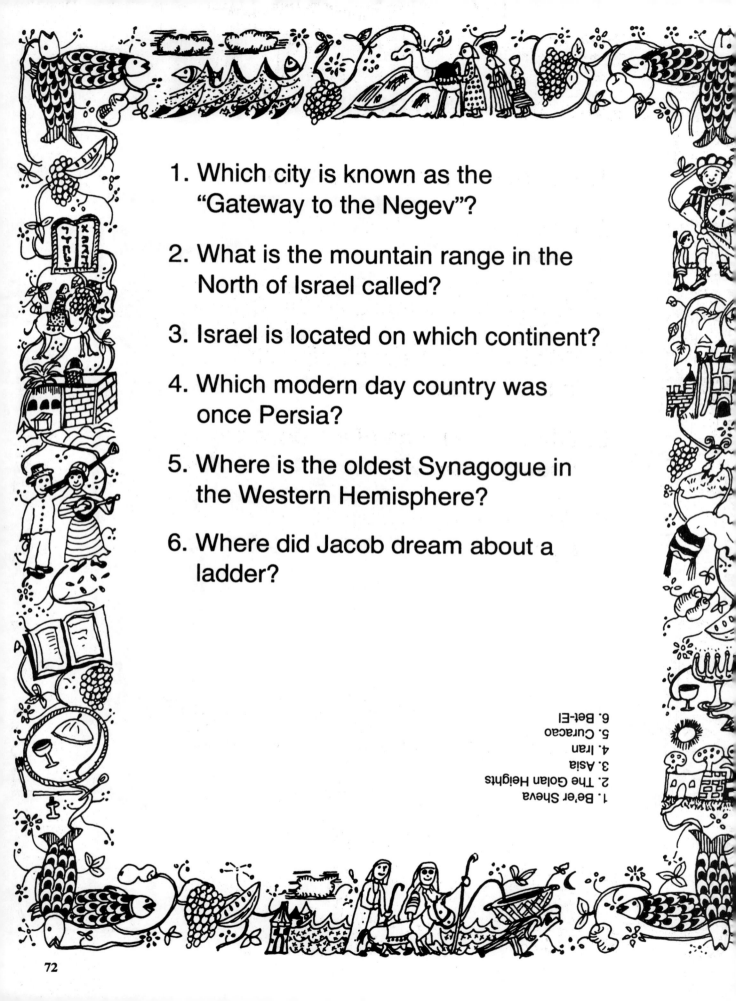

1. Which city is known as the "Gateway to the Negev"?

2. What is the mountain range in the North of Israel called?

3. Israel is located on which continent?

4. Which modern day country was once Persia?

5. Where is the oldest Synagogue in the Western Hemisphere?

6. Where did Jacob dream about a ladder?

1. Be'er Sheva
2. The Golan Heights
3. Asia
4. Iran
5. Curacao
6. Bet-El

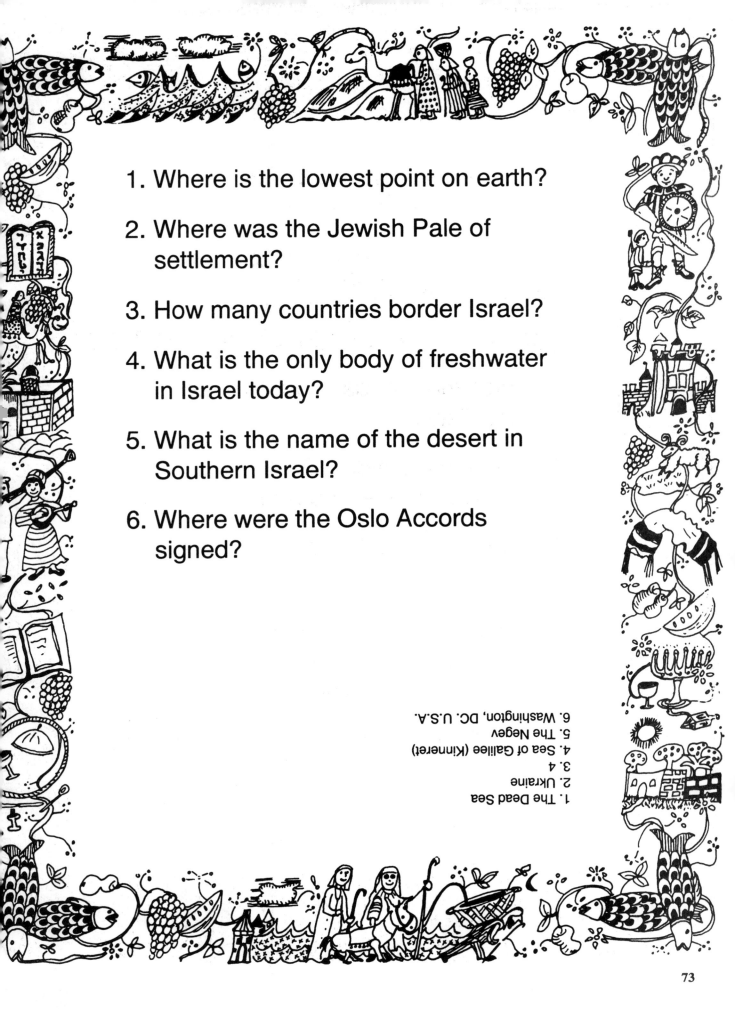

1. Where is the lowest point on earth?

2. Where was the Jewish Pale of settlement?

3. How many countries border Israel?

4. What is the only body of freshwater in Israel today?

5. What is the name of the desert in Southern Israel?

6. Where were the Oslo Accords signed?

1. The Dead Sea
2. Ukraine
3. 4
4. Sea of Galilee (Kinneret)
5. The Negev
6. Washington, DC. U.S.A.

1. In which city were the 1972 Israeli Olympic athletes murdered?

2. Where was the first Jewish Ghetto?

3. What is the name of Israel's highest mountain?

4. What is the largest city in Israel?

5. What famous scrolls were found in Qumran?

6. On which mountain is the main campus of the Hebrew University of Jerusalem?

1. Munich
2. Venice
3. Mount Hermon
4. Tel Aviv
5. The Dead Sea Scrolls
6. Mount Scopus

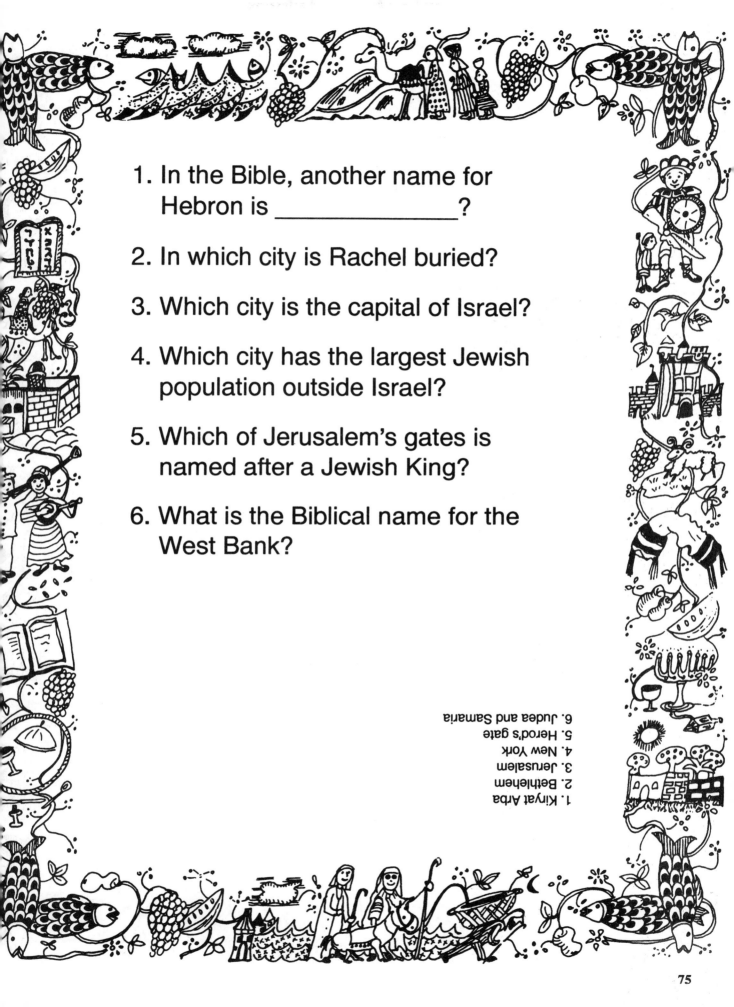

1. In the Bible, another name for Hebron is _____?

2. In which city is Rachel buried?

3. Which city is the capital of Israel?

4. Which city has the largest Jewish population outside Israel?

5. Which of Jerusalem's gates is named after a Jewish King?

6. What is the Biblical name for the West Bank?

1. Kiryat Arba
2. Bethlehem
3. Jerusalem
4. New York
5. Herod's gate
6. Judea and Samaria

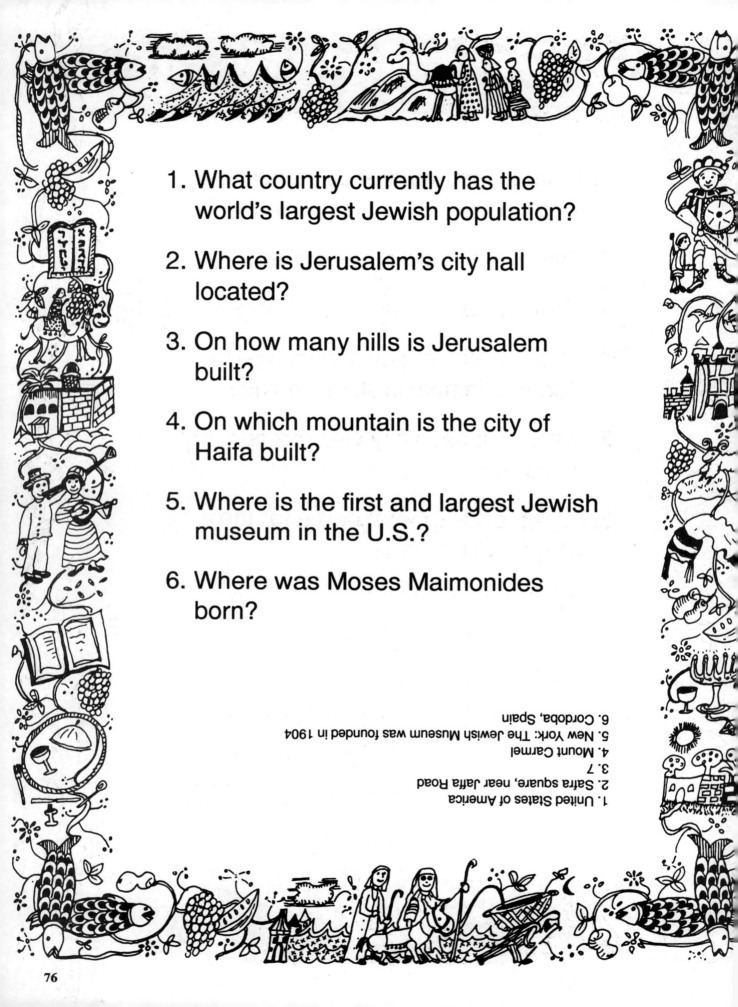

1. What country currently has the world's largest Jewish population?

2. Where is Jerusalem's city hall located?

3. On how many hills is Jerusalem built?

4. On which mountain is the city of Haifa built?

5. Where is the first and largest Jewish museum in the U.S.?

6. Where was Moses Maimonides born?

1. United States of America
2. Safra square, near Jaffa Road
3. 7
4. Mount Carmel
5. New York: The Jewish Museum was founded in 1904
6. Cordoba, Spain

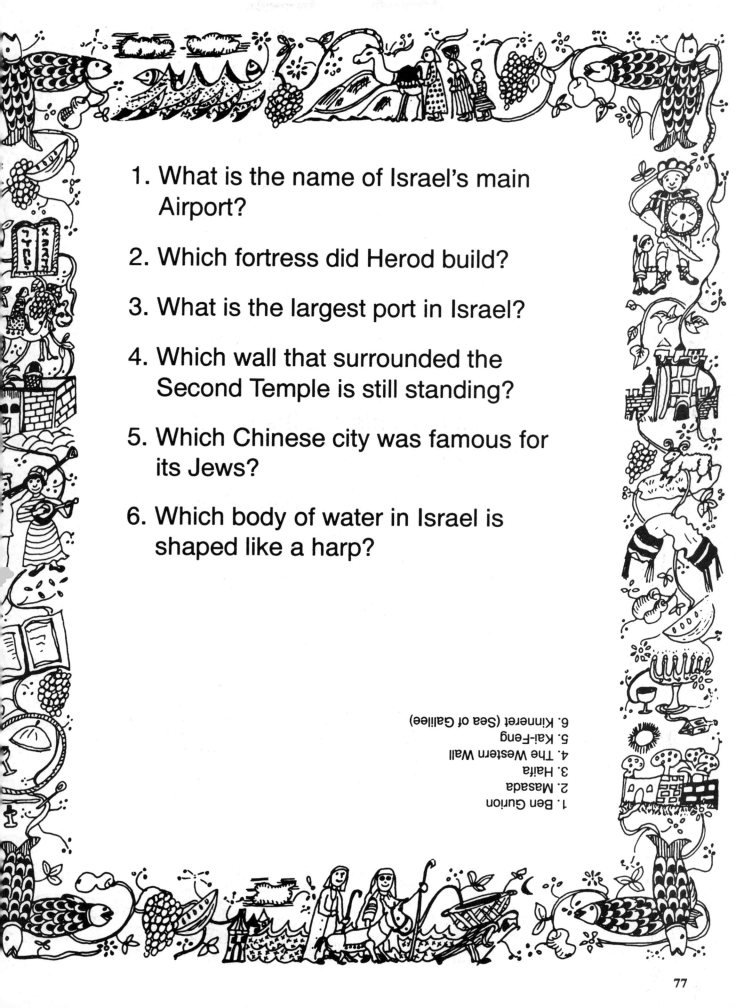

1. What is the name of Israel's main Airport?

2. Which fortress did Herod build?

3. What is the largest port in Israel?

4. Which wall that surrounded the Second Temple is still standing?

5. Which Chinese city was famous for its Jews?

6. Which body of water in Israel is shaped like a harp?

1. Ben Gurion
2. Masada
3. Haifa
4. The Western Wall
5. Kai-Feng
6. Kinneret (Sea of Galilee)

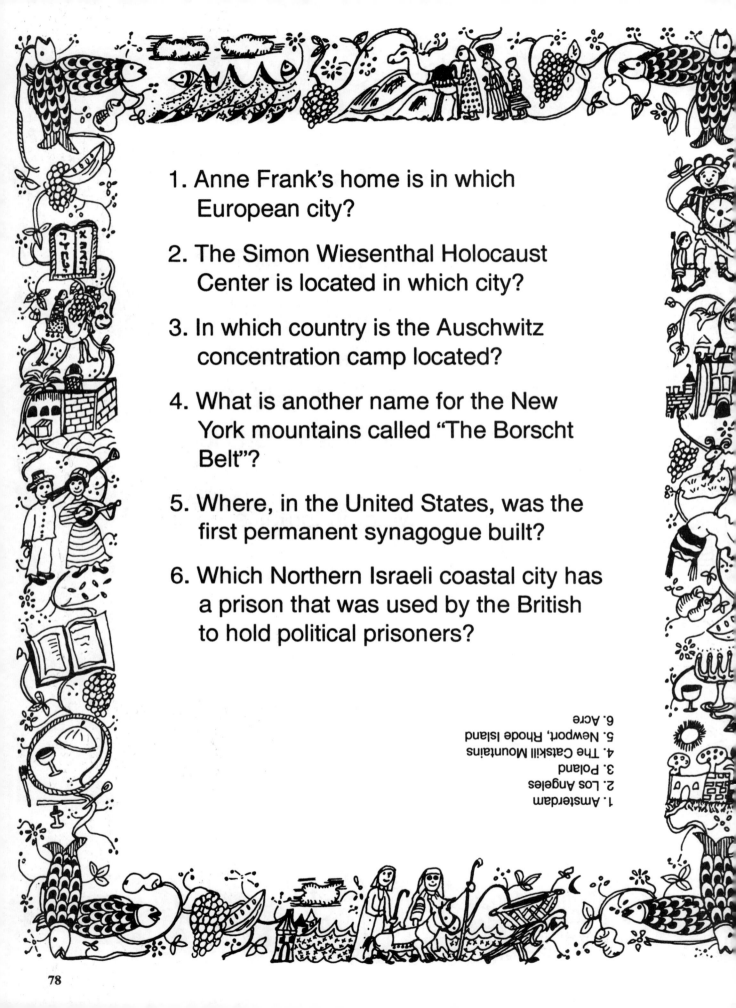

1. Anne Frank's home is in which European city?

2. The Simon Wiesenthal Holocaust Center is located in which city?

3. In which country is the Auschwitz concentration camp located?

4. What is another name for the New York mountains called "The Borscht Belt"?

5. Where, in the United States, was the first permanent synagogue built?

6. Which Northern Israeli coastal city has a prison that was used by the British to hold political prisoners?

1. Amsterdam
2. Los Angeles
3. Poland
4. The Catskill Mountains
5. Newport, Rhode Island
6. Acre

1. In which city is David buried?

2. In which area of Israel are Druse villages found?

3. Where, in Israel, is there a subway named the "Carmelit"?

4. In which city is the Tower of David found?

5. Which European city was made famous by its "Golem"?

6. In which Israeli city is Maimonides buried?

1. Jerusalem
2. The Galilee
3. Haifa
4. Jerusalem
5. Prague
6. Tiberias

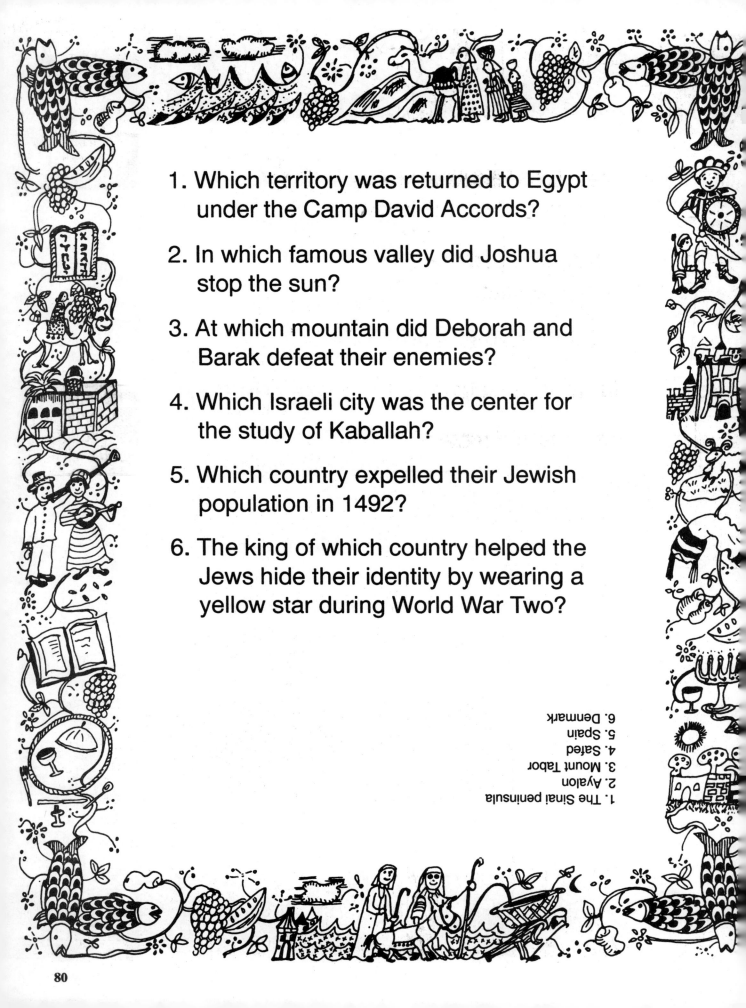

1. Which territory was returned to Egypt under the Camp David Accords?

2. In which famous valley did Joshua stop the sun?

3. At which mountain did Deborah and Barak defeat their enemies?

4. Which Israeli city was the center for the study of Kaballah?

5. Which country expelled their Jewish population in 1492?

6. The king of which country helped the Jews hide their identity by wearing a yellow star during World War Two?

1. The Sinai peninsula
2. Ayalon
3. Mount Tabor
4. Safed
5. Spain
6. Denmark

Jewish History

1. When was the city of Tel Aviv first built?

2. When did the Gulf War start?

3. What is the name of the first Kibbutz?

4. When were the Jews expelled from England?

5. Who wrote "I never saw another butterfly"?

6. Who killed John F. Kennedy's assassin?

1. 1909
2. January 19, 1991
3. Degania
4. 1290
5. The children of the Terezin concentration camp
6. Jack Ruby

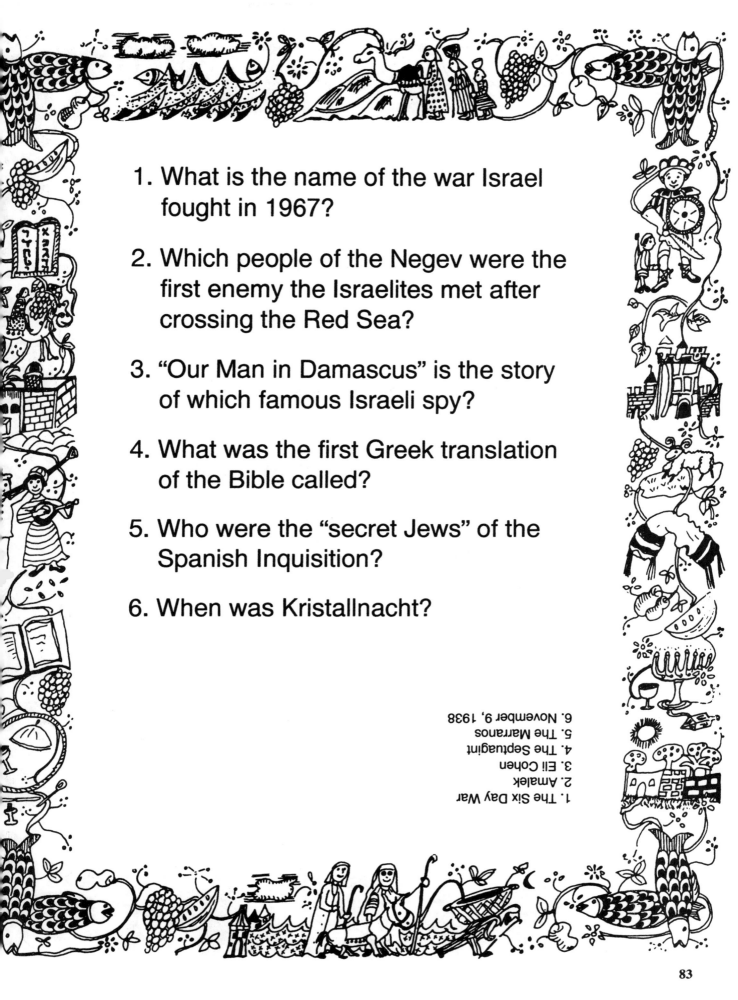

1. What is the name of the war Israel fought in 1967?

2. Which people of the Negev were the first enemy the Israelites met after crossing the Red Sea?

3. "Our Man in Damascus" is the story of which famous Israeli spy?

4. What was the first Greek translation of the Bible called?

5. Who were the "secret Jews" of the Spanish Inquisition?

6. When was Kristallnacht?

1. The Six Day War
2. Amalek
3. Eli Cohen
4. The Septuagint
5. The Marranos
6. November 9, 1938

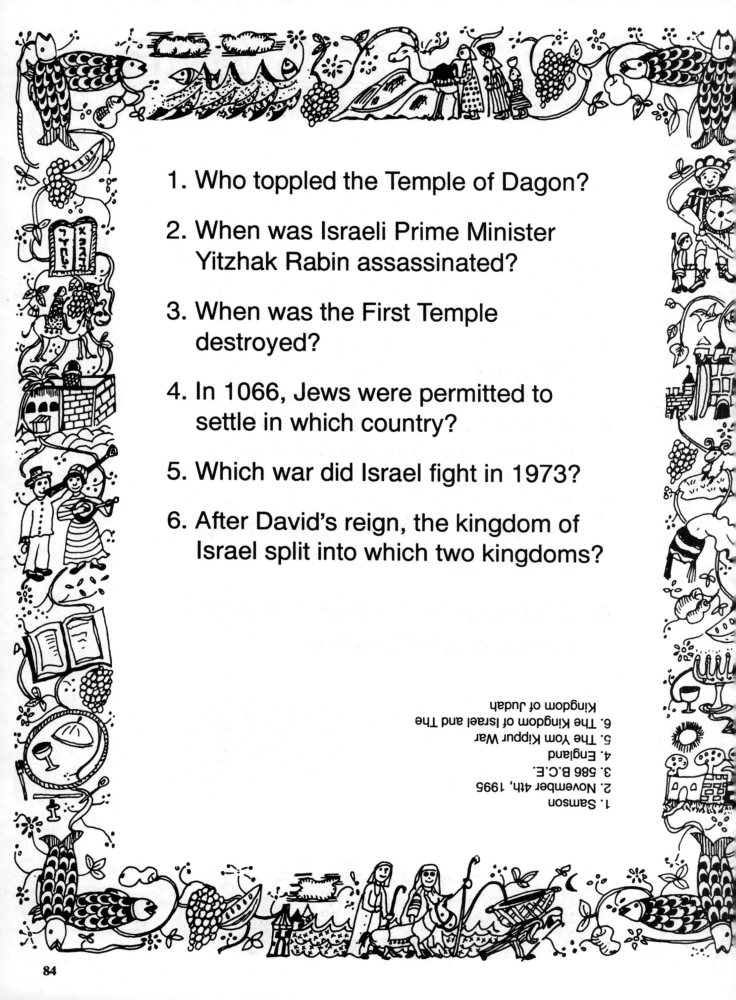

1. Who toppled the Temple of Dagon?

2. When was Israeli Prime Minister Yitzhak Rabin assassinated?

3. When was the First Temple destroyed?

4. In 1066, Jews were permitted to settle in which country?

5. Which war did Israel fight in 1973?

6. After David's reign, the kingdom of Israel split into which two kingdoms?

1. Samson
2. November 4th, 1995
3. 586 B.C.E.
4. England
5. The Yom Kippur War
6. The Kingdom of Israel and The Kingdom of Judah

1. Operation "Magic Carpet" brought the Jews of which country to Israel?

2. Who forbade polygamy for the Jews?

3. Which cities did the Israelites build in Egypt?

4. Who was the King of Israel when the First Temple was destroyed?

5. What fast day is named after the last ruler of Israel appointed by the Babylonians?

6. What name was given to the airlift of Ethiopian Jews to Israel?

1. Yemen
2. Rabbenu Gershon
3. Pithom and Ramses
4. King Zedekiah
5. The fast of Gedaliah
6. Operation Solomon

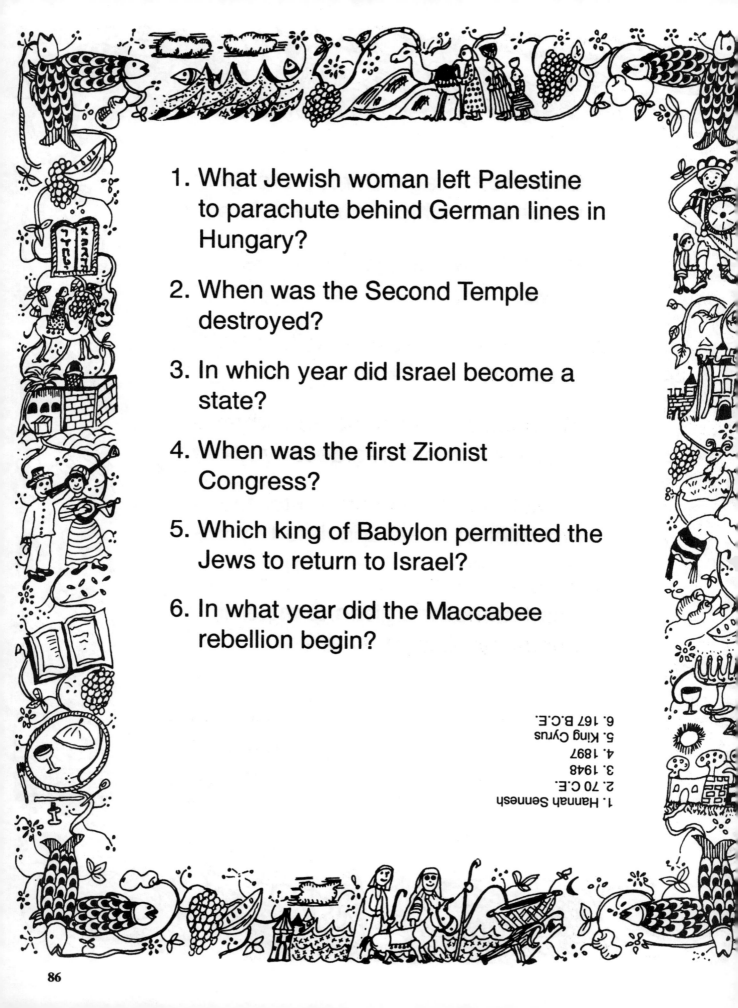

1. What Jewish woman left Palestine to parachute behind German lines in Hungary?

2. When was the Second Temple destroyed?

3. In which year did Israel become a state?

4. When was the first Zionist Congress?

5. Which king of Babylon permitted the Jews to return to Israel?

6. In what year did the Maccabee rebellion begin?

1. Hannah Senesh
2. 70 C.E.
3. 1948
4. 1897
5. King Cyrus
6. 167 B.C.E.

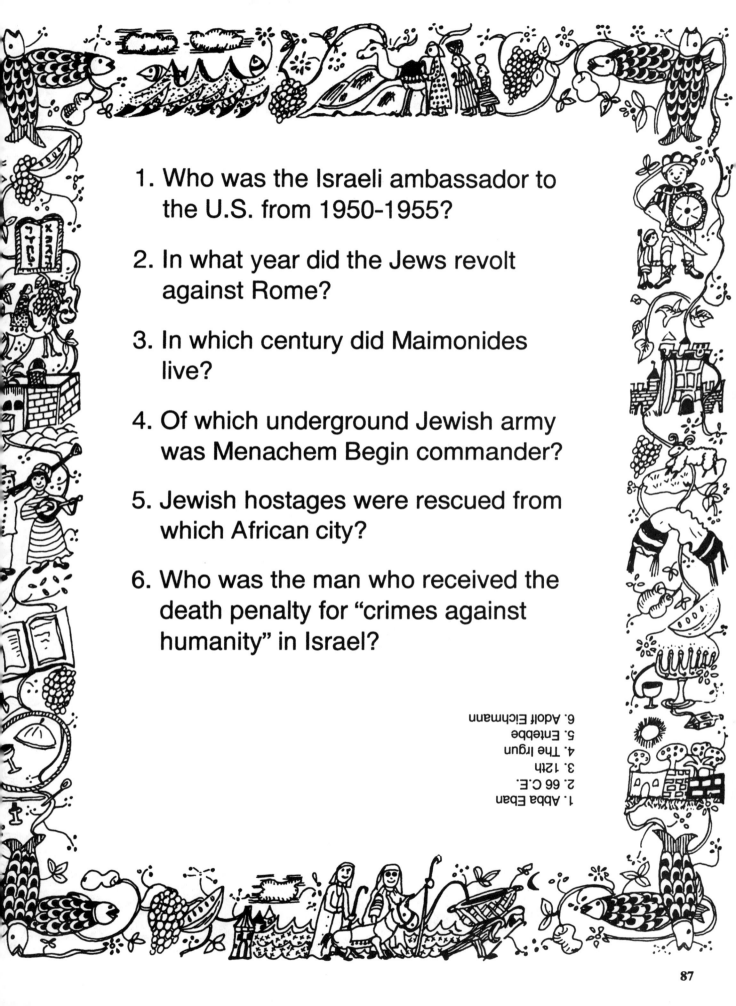

1. Who was the Israeli ambassador to the U.S. from 1950-1955?

2. In what year did the Jews revolt against Rome?

3. In which century did Maimonides live?

4. Of which underground Jewish army was Menachem Begin commander?

5. Jewish hostages were rescued from which African city?

6. Who was the man who received the death penalty for "crimes against humanity" in Israel?

1. Abba Eban
2. 66 C.E.
3. 12th
4. The Irgun
5. Entebbe
6. Adolf Eichmann

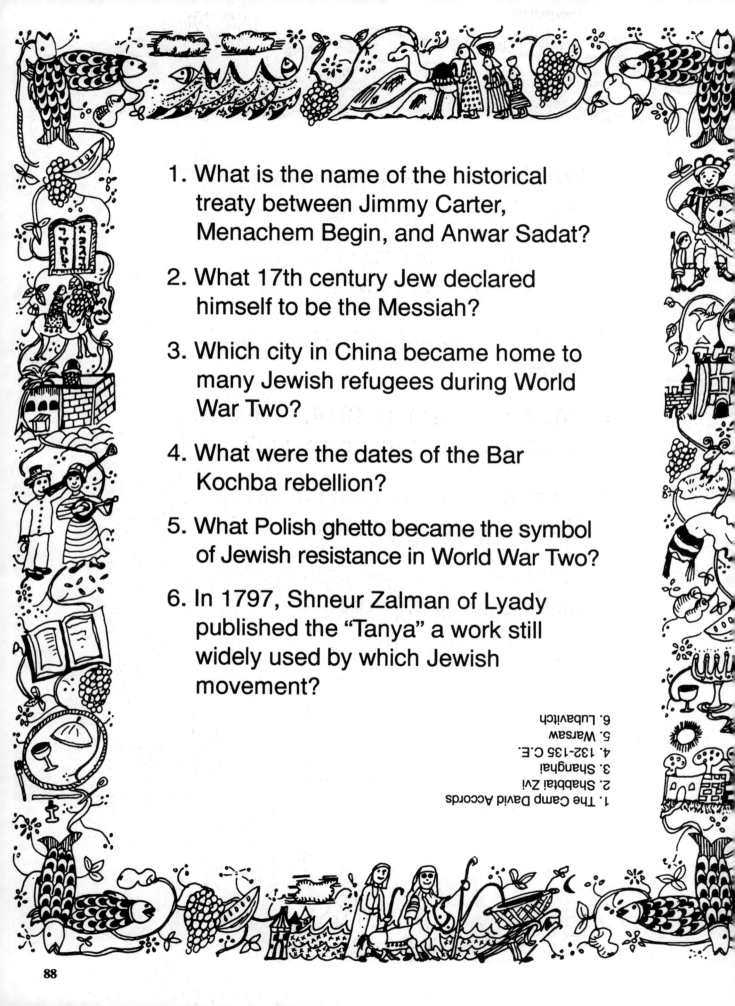

1. What is the name of the historical treaty between Jimmy Carter, Menachem Begin, and Anwar Sadat?

2. What 17th century Jew declared himself to be the Messiah?

3. Which city in China became home to many Jewish refugees during World War Two?

4. What were the dates of the Bar Kochba rebellion?

5. What Polish ghetto became the symbol of Jewish resistance in World War Two?

6. In 1797, Shneur Zalman of Lyady published the "Tanya" a work still widely used by which Jewish movement?

6. Lubavitch
5. Warsaw
4. 132-135 C.E.
3. Shanghai
2. Shabbtai Zvi
1. The Camp David Accords

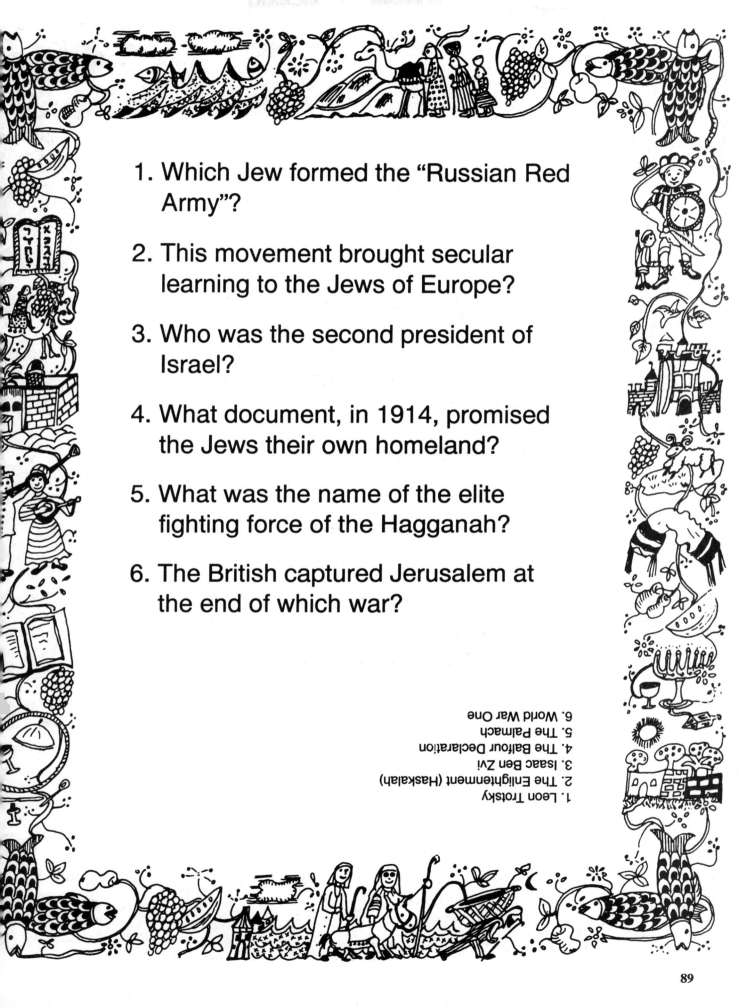

1. Which Jew formed the "Russian Red Army"?

2. This movement brought secular learning to the Jews of Europe?

3. Who was the second president of Israel?

4. What document, in 1914, promised the Jews their own homeland?

5. What was the name of the elite fighting force of the Hagganah?

6. The British captured Jerusalem at the end of which war?

1. Leon Trotsky
2. The Enlightenment (Haskalah)
3. Isaac Ben Zvi
4. The Balfour Declaration
5. The Palmach
6. World War One

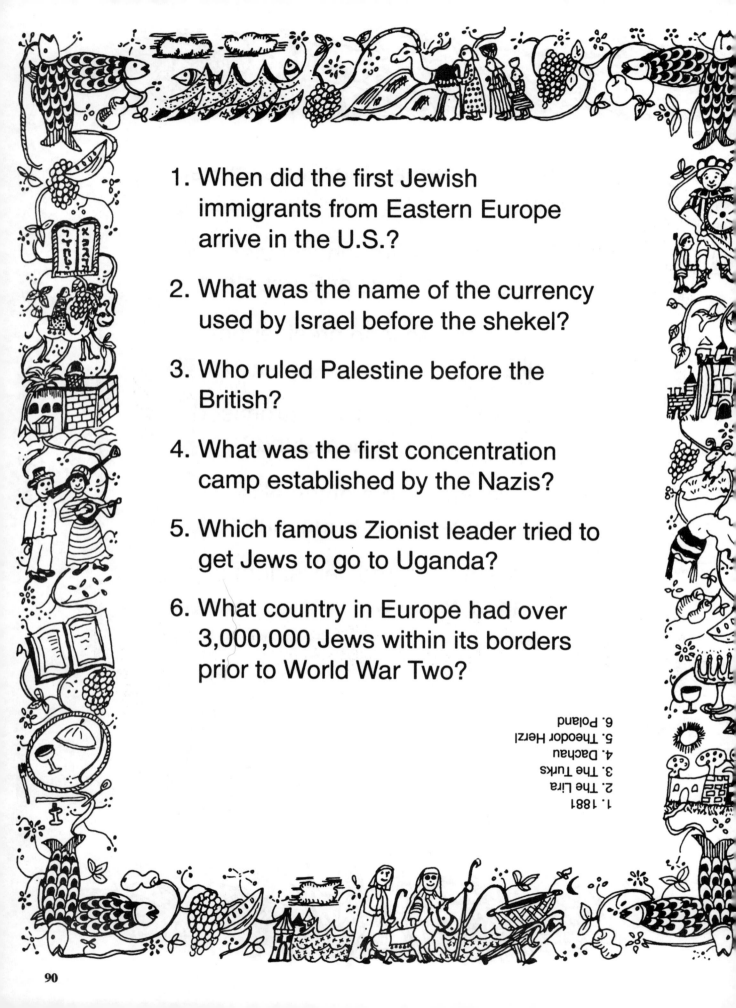

1. When did the first Jewish immigrants from Eastern Europe arrive in the U.S.?

2. What was the name of the currency used by Israel before the shekel?

3. Who ruled Palestine before the British?

4. What was the first concentration camp established by the Nazis?

5. Which famous Zionist leader tried to get Jews to go to Uganda?

6. What country in Europe had over 3,000,000 Jews within its borders prior to World War Two?

1. 1881
2. The Lira
3. The Turks
4. Dachau
5. Theodor Herzl
6. Poland

My Jewish Name Means...

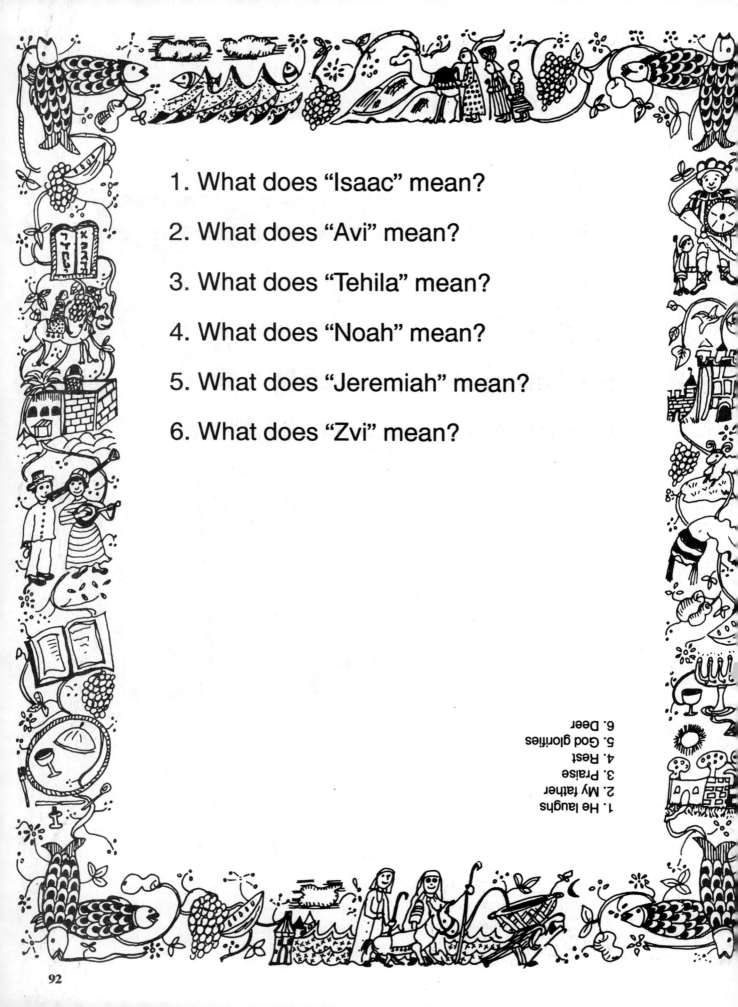

1. What does "Isaac" mean?

2. What does "Avi" mean?

3. What does "Tehila" mean?

4. What does "Noah" mean?

5. What does "Jeremiah" mean?

6. What does "Zvi" mean?

1. He laughs
2. My father
3. Praise
4. Rest
5. God glorifies
6. Deer

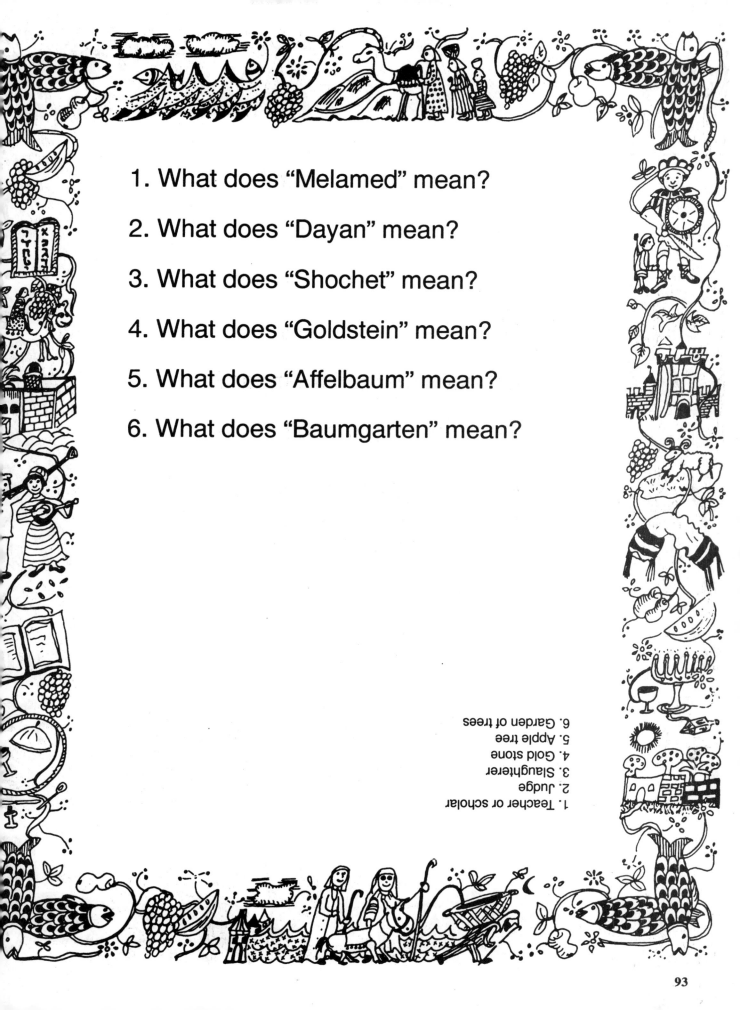

1. What does "Melamed" mean?

2. What does "Dayan" mean?

3. What does "Shochet" mean?

4. What does "Goldstein" mean?

5. What does "Affelbaum" mean?

6. What does "Baumgarten" mean?

1. Teacher or scholar
2. Judge
3. Slaughterer
4. Gold stone
5. Apple tree
6. Garden of trees

1. What does "Mandelbaum" mean?

2. What does "Weiss" mean?

3. What does "Schwartz" mean?

4. What does "Lieberman" mean?

5. "Yaakov" comes from the word "ekev" because he grabbed on to his brother's _____?

6. "Adam" was named after "adama" which means _____ because that is what he was made from?

1. Almond tree
2. White
3. Black
4. Friend
5. Heel
6. Earth

94

1. What does "Raphael" mean?

2. What does "Michael" mean?

3. What does "Abigail" mean?

4. what does "Hadassah" mean?

5. What does "Solomon" mean?

6. What does "Joshua" mean?

1. God has healed
2. Who is God like
3. My father is joyous
4. Myrtle tree
5. Peaceable
6. God saves

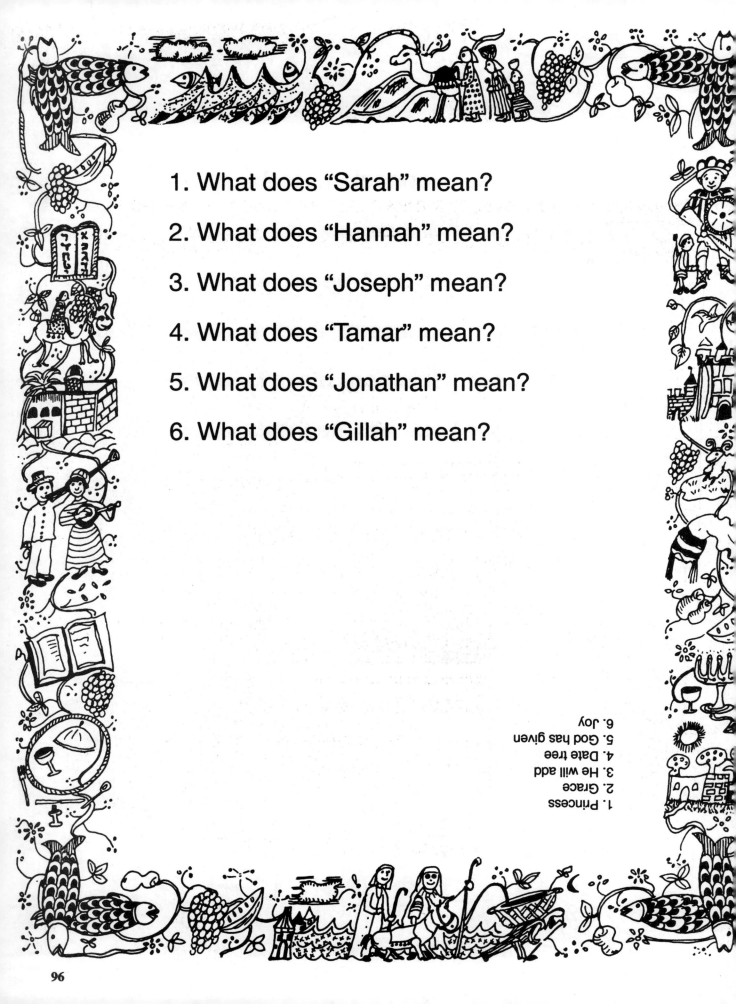

1. What does "Sarah" mean?

2. What does "Hannah" mean?

3. What does "Joseph" mean?

4. What does "Tamar" mean?

5. What does "Jonathan" mean?

6. What does "Gillah" mean?

1. Princess
2. Grace
3. He will add
4. Date tree
5. God has given
6. Joy